Dissertation Skills

for Business and Management Students 2e

Brian White
and
Stephen Rayner

CENGAGE
Learning

Australia • Brazil • Japan • Korea • Mexico • Singapore • Spain • United Kingdom • United States

CENGAGE
Learning·

Dissertation Skills for Business and Management Students, 2e

Brian White and Stephen Rayner

Publishing Director: Linden Harris

Publisher: Andrew Ashwin

Senior Production Editor: Alison Burt

Editorial Assistant: Jennifer Grene

Senior Manufacturing Buyer: Eyvett Davis

Marketing Executive: Amanda Cheung

Typesetter: MPS Limited

Cover design: Adam Renvoize

For product information and technology assistance, contact **emea.info@cengage.com**. For permission to use material from this text or product, and for permission queries, email **emea.permissions@cengage.com**.

British Library Cataloguing-in-Publication Data
A catalogue record for this book is available from the British Library.

ISBN: 978-1-4080-8177-8

Cengage Learning EMEA
Cheriton House, North Way, Andover, Hampshire, SP10 5BE United Kingdom

Cengage Learning products are represented in Canada by Nelson Education Ltd.

For your lifelong learning solutions, visit **www.cengage.co.uk**

Purchase your next print book, e-book or e-chapter at **www.cengagebrain.com**

Printed in China by RR Donnelley
1 2 3 4 5 6 7 8 9 10 – 16 15 14

Contents

Acknowledgements

The authors would like to thank all the staff at Cengage for their professional advice. In particular we would like to mention Jenny Grene and Felix Rowe for sound advice and guidance at all stages in the writing and publication.

Brian White would also like to give a special thank you to his wife Margaret at the word processing and proofreading stages. Also thanks to his son Matthew, and daughter-in-law Helen, for help with Chapter 7. It was much appreciated.

The publishers would like to thank the reviewers for their constructive comments during the writing of the book.

Shaukat Ali, University of Wolverhampton

Maryam Alshahrani, University of Wolverhampton

Mohammed Kara, University of Johannesburg

Rachael Morris, Newcastle Business School

Nicola Patterson, Newcastle Business School

Bernadette Warner, London School of Commerce

Preface

The first edition of this book was published in 2000 and this was followed with a special MBA version in 2002. Both books have sold well and the comments received from students who used the books have been very favourable, with many commenting that the books really helped them with their dissertations.

However, while many of the central issues concerned with dissertations remain the same today, there have been changes in the last ten years that this updated edition reflects. This new edition also combines all academic levels and will be equally useful to undergraduate and postgraduate students.

Although the basic layout and structure has been retained, each chapter has been carefully reviewed by Brian White and Stephen Rayner. For example, Chapter 7 about using the literature has been revised to take more account of the Internet as a source of information. The chapters on the processes of research discuss in more depth the philosophical underpinning involved in research. Both authors hope this new book will help students succeed in the production of a good dissertation.

Brian White
Stephen Rayner
July 2013

1   What this book is about

Introduction

The aim of this book is to help you, the student, produce a successful dissertation.

Also known by other names such as elective study, management project, long essay, extended essay, a dissertation is a long and extensive piece of independent work. If you are enrolled on a Doctorate programme the term 'thesis' is often used. In reality all these terms may be regarded as the same, and throughout this book the term 'dissertation' will be used. This book will use the word 'university' to include universities, institutes and colleges of higher education that are eligible to award degrees.

In this chapter some basic concepts about dissertations are introduced. They include what a dissertation is, the place of dissertations on degree programmes, how this book can help you and what the characteristic features of a dissertation are. The value of dissertations, the skills you need, and the important role of supervisors are also discussed.

What is a dissertation?

Let's start by asking the very basic but important question–what is a dissertation? It is not an essay; nor is it an ordinary business, management, consultancy or market research report. So what is it?

Different authors provide varying definitions, but for our purpose a dissertation can be defined as a long piece of formal academic writing, divided into headed sections or chapters. You will research, in detail, a particular business or management subject, which you will normally choose yourself. On your own, you will investigate areas which, in some respects, may be entirely new and unfamiliar to you. You will be expected to critique your work with that of other researchers and discuss the various theories involved. To do this successfully you will need to collect a lot of information. You will use libraries, the Internet and, depending on the topic, may carry out your own research to collect new material. Having collected the information and data, you then have to interpret what it all means, and write it up in an accepted academic format. The final dissertation must demonstrate originality, and evidence of academic criticism and analysis.

Not surprisingly, even the most able student can find the dissertation a daunting experience. Don't be put off. A dissertation provides you with a unique opportunity to demonstrate your academic skills. It gives you the chance to study in detail a subject in which you have a genuine interest, and this in itself can give a great sense of personal satisfaction. It demonstrates, more than anything else, your ability to carry out successfully a significant piece of independent work.

The role of dissertations on undergraduate and postgraduate courses

Students study in a variety of ways and circumstances. You may be on a full-time, part-time, flexible or distance learning course, but irrespective of all of these considerations, you may still need to produce a dissertation. The precise length and nature of the dissertation will depend on the course and whether you are enrolled on either an undergraduate or postgraduate degree. Let's consider each in turn.

Undergraduate courses

Most undergraduate business and management degree students (e.g. BA Business Studies) are required, usually in their final year, to produce a dissertation. It forms an important part of the final year, and is a substantial part of the total assessment. At some universities the dissertation is the key factor which influences the student's final degree classification. It can determine whether you receive a first, second or third class degree. It makes good sense, therefore, to approach your dissertation in a positive way. Regard it as a challenge. Look on it as an opportunity to demonstrate how good you are; it provides a way to produce a piece of work that sets you apart from the other students. However, the thought of having to write a 10 000 to 12 000-word dissertation (at some universities the length can be up to 20 000 words) often causes the most able undergraduate student to feel undue apprehension and anxiety. In fact, the first word which comes to mind for many students when faced with the task of starting a dissertation is *HELP*! Hopefully this book will provide the extra help you need.

Postgraduate courses

Students at postgraduate level also have to produce dissertations and may be enrolled on either a Masters or Doctorate programme.

Students studying for a Masters degree in business and management are normally enrolled on either a MBA (Master of Business Administration) or MSc (Master of Science) degree. MScs are available in a variety of subjects including Advertising and Marketing, Business Management, Education Management, Banking and Finance, e-Business and Leisure Management.

The subject content of the different degree programmes varies. The majority begin with a core curriculum which includes the generic areas of business and management, for example, marketing, finance, human resource management or strategic management. In the final part of a Masters programme students usually have to carry out an independent piece of research and write it up as a dissertation. As with undergraduate courses the length can vary, but is usually between 15 000 and 40 000 words. Also, as with Bachelor degrees, the dissertation is usually the largest piece of assessed work and may make up 40 per cent of the final mark. It usually determines whether the Masters degree is awarded at pass, merit or distinction level.

Doctorate students also have to produce dissertations. Nowadays in universities, two types of Doctorate programme are usually available.

Firstly, there is the traditional PhD (Doctor of Philosophy) degree. This is purely a research-based degree, and the student studies in great depth one particular subject, and at the end produces a dissertation that can be well over 100 000 words. Full-time PhD students normally take approximately three years to produce their work, and part-time students somewhere between five to seven years. The actual time varies with each university.

Secondly, degrees termed professional Doctorates are available. These include the DBA (Doctor of Business Administration), and the EdD (Doctor of Education) programmes. Available in many countries, professional Doctorates began to appear in UK universities in the 1990s. There is normally a taught element at the beginning of the programme, and this is followed by the students having to produce a dissertation towards the end. The standard of a taught doctoral programme is the same as that of the traditional PhD degree, but because there is an assessed taught element the length of the dissertation is less, but it still can be in the region of 50 000 and 70 000 words.

How this book can help

Irrespective of whether you are on a Bachelors, Masters, or Doctorate degree the stages you go through to produce a dissertation are the same. Obviously with a Masters degree each stage is more detailed and thorough, and this is further increased at Doctorate level. The different academic levels are achieved with each degree in that more time is devoted at each stage in order to attain a greater breadth and depth of the topic being researched. With higher degrees, for example the PhD, the literature review has to be more exhaustive and the research design more rigorous. A greater insight into the role of theory and academic analysis and criticism is required.

This book has been written, therefore, to provide the positive and practical help you need. It covers all the main stages in the production of a dissertation and includes topics such as:

- establishing a good working relationship with your supervisor;
- choosing an area to study and deciding on the title;
- deciding what is research and how the chosen topic applies to business and management;
- writing a suitable research proposal;
- selecting the best research methodological approach(es) to use;
- using libraries and the Internet for the collection and evaluation of published information;
- collecting, by various research methods and techniques, your own information and data;
- evaluating and analyzing the information and data you collect;
- writing up the dissertation and choosing the most appropriate layout;
- the assessment of dissertations, including (if required) a *viva* examination and presentation.

In addition, certain basic questions like 'What is the value of a dissertation?' are answered, together with advice about the necessary study and research skills you need when starting a dissertation. Consideration is given to the ethical issues you need to think about with business and management research and, at the end of the book, an annotated bibliography (page 210) is included in case you need extra help in a particular area. A glossary of terms associated with research and dissertation is also included.

Although this book takes you through the stages of preparing and writing a dissertation it does not cover the administrative and organizational requirements of individual universities. Each university should provide this sort of detail in course handbooks, etc. Most business degree programmes have course leaders, year tutors or dissertation supervisors who provide information about hand-in dates, regulations and other information about your course. Many universities, on their websites, provide general guidance on research and dissertation preparation. Make use of them.

The characteristic features of a dissertation

In order to produce a dissertation you must have effective study and research skills. Before the skills you need are discussed it may help to explain the characteristic features of a dissertation. This will give you a better idea of exactly what is involved.

- *A dissertation is an independent piece of work.* Although all your assignments, either on this or other courses you have attended, are independent pieces of work, in that you do them on your own and without **plagiarism**, a dissertation is truly independent because no other student is working on the same topic. With other assignments many students may be working on the same title. This means that a dissertation gives you a chance to show how good you really are. A dissertation is an excellent indicator of a student's true ability, and can help with your final degree classification.

- *A dissertation shows detailed knowledge and understanding.* Dissertations require a lot of information. This means you have to spend a long time collecting and searching out relevant material. You need to demonstrate a thorough knowledge of the literature and be able to discuss the theoretical concepts of the topic.

- *A dissertation needs organization and good planning.* Because a dissertation is long, it takes time to complete and you need to be able to organize and plan the work over an extended period, sometimes between 6 and 9 months on Bachelors and Masters programmes, although students on doctoral programmes have far more time. Your ability to plan work independently over such a long period again demonstrates why dissertations are often included in courses. It makes you responsible for your own learning. Students on part-time and distance learning programmes also need to balance the dissertation workload with pressures of home life, family and career.

- *A dissertation shows critical and analytical thinking.* Too many dissertations are spoilt because students simply describe situations. You must be prepared to question, identify trends and provide evidence to support your ideas. If you have carried out research, you must defend your research design and data collection techniques. You must subject your work, and that of others, to serious questioning, rather than just accepting it at face value. It is important to relate theory with practice.

- *A dissertation illustrates the context of existing knowledge.* It is important that a literature review is included which collates previously published work in the same field. Your dissertation is not an isolated investigation. You need to show how it relates to what other people have done. Again, other people's work must not simply be described. It is the relationship between your work and theirs which demonstrates criticism and analysis. This is especially important at higher degree (e.g. PhD) level.

- *A dissertation has a high standard of communication and presentation.* Good English, correct spelling and grammar are essential. Moreover, the work must look neat on the page. Sloppy, untidy and inaccurate work can make a dissertation fail. It is essential to produce a professional looking document. A dissertation must also be prepared according to an accepted format, so check your course regulations.
- *A dissertation demonstrates original work and research.* Students often think that their work must be as original as Einstein's theory of relativity. Unfortunately, very few of us have the flair and intellect of Einstein. By original work and research, we mean that you should put forward your own ideas and back them up with appropriate evidence. This might be generated as a result of a questionnaire, interview, or other data collecting techniques. Alternatively, you might use published information, and present it in a different and new manner, which in itself is original. The emphasis again is on critical and analytical thinking; a description of either your own or other people's work without some analysis and discussion is not enough.
- *A dissertation has an academic approach.* A dissertation presents a well-evidenced argument. The evidence cited is the research of others, your own, or usually a combination of both. It needs to be sound and collected in an ordered, logical fashion. A dissertation is an academic document and must have an appropriate format following accepted conventions of referencing styles. It should always include a **bibliography**. Normally it is written in a very formal style using the third person.

Value of a dissertation
Academic value

For many undergraduate, and some postgraduate students, the dissertation is the first truly independent piece of work they complete. Although all your degree work is your own in terms of academic integrity and the absence of plagiarism, with the present-day emphasis on group work and everyone in large classes doing the same assignments, students get few chances to work completely on their own. The value of a dissertation is that it allows you to demonstrate, in a very positive way, that you can work alone. It gives you, the student, an opportunity to show your true worth.

If you are on a Bachelors or Masters degree the dissertation is an important part of the final stage of your degree. Many lecturers would argue that it reflects, more than anything else you do on a course, your true intellectual ability. Certainly, it often gives a clear indication of the degree classification the student should be awarded. For example, imagine you are a lecturer attending a BA Business Studies examination board and a student's degree classification, based on four pieces of assessed work and the dissertation is being decided. The student has one piece of work with an upper second class mark (e.g. 61 per cent) and three pieces with lower second class marks (e.g. 58 per cent, 57 per cent and 59 per cent). This student is borderline, so what final degree class would the student be awarded? In most cases the board would look at the dissertation mark, and if this was well in the upper second category (e.g. 67 per cent); the chances are the student would be given an upper second class degree. Conversely, if the mark was in the low fifties (e.g. 53 per cent), the student would, most likely, receive a lower second class degree.

On a Masters programme the dissertation can contribute somewhere in the region of 40 per cent of the total assessment. Masters programmes are usually graded at pass, merit or distinction. Certain universities require the dissertation mark for distinction to be 70 per cent or over. It makes sense, therefore, to give the dissertation your best shot.

PhD and professional Doctorate students may be awarded their degrees purely on the quality of their dissertation, and how they respond to questions in a *viva* examination. The assessment of dissertations is discussed in some detail in Chapter 10 (page 174).

Personal and career value

In addition to academic importance, dissertations help with your personal and career development. As the dissertation comes towards the end of a degree programme it assesses a whole range of skills and competencies. The process of producing and writing a dissertation develops some very important skills that potential employers always require. These are termed 'personal transferable skills' and include things like planning, organizing, analyzing, criticizing, information gathering, identifying and solving problems, logical thinking, time management, data interpretation, research methods, and communication skills such as writing. A dissertation is something you can take with you to an interview to show to a prospective employer. It indicates that you can work independently to produce a substantial piece of work. In summary, it is tangible evidence that reflects your true academic ability.

Many Masters and Doctorate students are part-time and already in business and management positions. For these students a dissertation provides the opportunity to study a real-life problem at work. You may, for example, be able to produce an in-company dissertation, which may lead to better informed business decisions in your organization. This will give you a sharper insight into what is happening. It may help you personally when viewed from your senior manager's position if promotions are being discussed.

Producing a dissertation – the stages involved

There are a number of stages involved in the production of a dissertation and these are summarized in Figure 1.1. In reality, once you start a dissertation several things seem to happen at once – you may be designing a questionnaire, reading some recent articles, waiting for an inter-library loan order, seeing your supervisor, and so on. Good and effective time management and organization skills are essential.

Depending on your topic, the time spent on each stage will vary. The way you plan your work should take into account your complete workload. Remember, depending on your course, there may be other assignments to complete in addition to the dissertation, alongside family and personal commitments. Try and put everything in perspective. Every so often stand back and review what is happening overall. The process of critical reflection is essential when working on a dissertation. Critical refection is mentioned again in Chapter 3 (page 27).

The study and research skills you need

A good dissertation is not written overnight. It takes time, considerable planning and effort. Mention has already been made of some of the intellectual and practical skills needed and these are further discussed below.

- *Library and information retrieval skills* (see Chapter 7, page 106). Dissertations require a great deal of information so be sure you know how to use libraries and the Internet to search for the material you need. Be aware of the information services (e.g. inter-library loans) that may be available. Keep detailed citation records of everything you read. Either use cards, set up a computer database or use a special software package. Associated with the collection of material is the way you use and evaluate it to inform the literature review and the overall research design of the dissertation. Information retrieval work involves a great deal of reading. If you think you read slowly, try out skim and rapid reading techniques – they do help. Certain books cited in the bibliography will help here.
- *Writing and note-taking skills* (see Chapter 9, page 154). Dissertations involve a lot of writing. Before you start, decide on the required format and the method of acknowledging and referencing other people's work. Decide

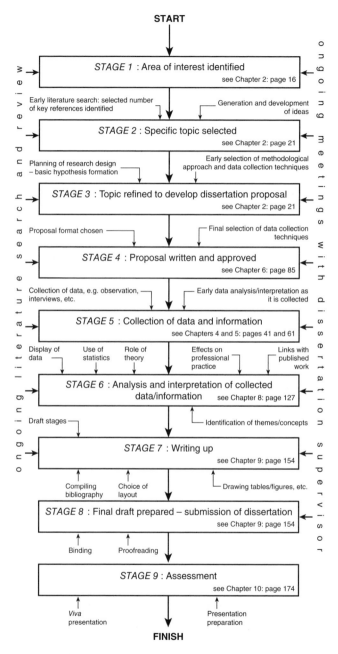

Figure 1.1 The stages involved in producing a dissertation

how to lay out the bibliography of the finished dissertation. Certain universities provide style manuals and handbooks – always follow their advice. When reading and making notes, be sure you are doing just that and not simply copying out large chunks of text. You will only have to sort it out later. You may as well do it at the start. With note making use a system you have used before and feel confident with. There are software packages on the market that can help with information management. Two examples are Mendeley and EndNote. EndNote helps manage your references, sorts out bibliographies, and searches databases, etc.

- *Research skills* (see Chapters 4, page 41 and 5, page 61). Dissertations need new information and data. The approach you take and the methods you select to collect information are as important as the material you collect. A sound **methodology** explained with reasons gives your work credibility. It means the results collected and conclusions arrived at are more valid and academically sound. Research skills also include data handling and interpretation. For qualitative research there are a number of Computer Assisted Qualitative Research Data Analysis Systems (CAQDAS) products on the market, including NVivo and ATLAS.ti. For statistical and quantitative analysis, products like IBM SPSS Statistics and Minitab are available. EndNote and Mendeley are noted above. If you think you are going to need any of these special software packages practise using them early. Be sure you know exactly what the programs are doing and you understand the underlying principles involved. The packages are expensive, but most universities subscribe and have a licence for student use.

- *Personal skills.* These include self-motivation, self-discipline, time management, and the ability to plan and organize. In short, these skills are all about being independent and taking responsibility for you own work and decisions. Many postgraduate students already possess an undergraduate degree, or equivalent, and have some work experience. Use this to your advantage. Reflect back and decide what your particular academic strengths are. What are you good at, and what do you find especially satisfying and motivating? Use this experience to the full. If you are a part-time or distance learning student working mainly off-campus, it is essential that you have the confidence to take responsibility for your own learning. Even though you will have the support of your supervisor and have contact, for example, by email, be prepared to spend a great deal of time working alone.

- *IT skills.* In recent years, with the expansion of the Internet and software development, the ability to use computers is an essential skill. You will use the Internet a great deal in searching out literature, handling software to analyze research results, producing and presenting presentations, and finally word-processing your final dissertation. Universities normally hold workshops and have a number of software packages for new students to introduce and/or update them to the world of IT. Commercial software development, and the Internet are changing all the time; it is essential to keep as up to date as possible.

The role of supervisors

Although the dissertation is an independent piece of work, universities realize that students need support in its preparation and writing up. In most institutions you will be allocated a supervisor; a member of the teaching staff who will help and advise you. Once you are allocated your supervisor it is your responsibility to contact them, as they don't normally chase up students. See your supervisor regularly and establish a good, professional working relationship. Many students don't do this and the lack of useful advice often results in a poor dissertation. Simple things like keeping appointments, doing any set tasks and getting work in on time all help. Remember that staff usually supervise a number of students on top of a teaching, administrative and research workload. Students, therefore, turning up unannounced expecting the red carpet treatment are not welcome. When you see your supervisor for the first time, agree between you whether it is better to have meetings weekly, fortnightly or monthly, etc. Decide together how to keep in contact, e.g. by telephone, emails, video link, etc. It is essential, from the beginning, that you develop an effective working relationship with your super-visor. As mentioned above, part-time students may work a great deal off-campus so it is very important that you and your supervisor agree a way to keep in con-tact. This way you can get feedback about your work and any likely problems can be identified and sorted out early on. As your dissertation progresses you may need to see your supervisor more or less frequently, depending on your needs. Lecturers realize this, since most of them at some time have written their own dissertations, and, as a result, are usually more than willing to accommodate the hard-working, motivated student. Regard the meetings with your supervisor as a real chance to engage in some meaningful academic debate.

In certain universities meetings between student and supervisor can be very formal and supervision codes of practice are published. These universities nor-mally expect supervisors and students to agree to a formal learning contract (sometimes termed '**learning agreement**'). Following each meeting notes are made or a form filled in to record the points discussed. In some universities the record is signed by supervisor and student, with a copy given to the student and one put into the student's file. Depending on your university the record of meetings, over the course of your dissertation, is presented to an examination board as part of your assessment.

At other universities a more informal process occurs. In this situation it's a good idea to write down, at the end of each supervisory meeting, a summary of the points discussed, and what specific things you need to do before the next session. Between visits draft an informal agenda of issues to discuss next time.

The following section highlights what supervisors will and will not do. Possibly another way of looking at this is what students expect of their supervisors and what supervisors expect of their students.

What supervisors will normally do

- Encourage you to do well.
- Help and support you when things go wrong.
- Identify gaps in your knowledge and help you to put them right.
- Identify extra skills that you need and advise on how to acquire them.
- Advise on planning, methodology and the interpretation of results.
- Check and monitor progress by reading and commenting on drafts of chapters and sections of the dissertation. Remember: it takes time to read a dissertation; so give them plenty of time to understand and comment on your work.
- Remind you of dates when work has to be finished.
- Open doors by introducing you to other members of staff who may give specific help with certain parts or chapters requiring specialist treatment, like data analysis or statistics.
- Be constructively critical of the work and offer helpful suggestions. However, be prepared to challenge new ideas and defend your own!

What supervisors won't do

- The work! It is your dissertation, not theirs.
- Write the dissertation for you. Supervisors will read sections and comment on general points, for example, how the argument is constructed, but don't expect them to re-write every sentence, or correct misspellings and grammatical errors.
- Do all the worrying. Supervisors are naturally concerned when things start to go wrong, and will try and help the conscientious, hard-working student. However, if you lack motivation and have a couldn't-care-less attitude, don't be surprised if you get a somewhat cool reception the next time you contact your supervisor.

- Give orders. Supervisors will suggest how to approach a problem and may indicate the advantages and limitations of particular methods and approaches. They expect you to consider their advice seriously, but they respect that the student has the final decision.

A word of warning

In recent years a number of websites have appeared on the Internet that claim to do a lot of the work for you. For a fee they will write your proposal, sort out your methodology, proofread your work and even write your dissertation. You can now buy a ready-made dissertation off the shelf. Not surprisingly most universities regard this sort of help as plagiarism and against their regulations. The advice would be: do not use these websites. If you come across anything where you are uncertain always talk it through with your supervisor. Note also that software is now available (eg. Turnitin) that can detect bought and plagiarized work – many universities use it to check a student's work before it is assessed, or as an actual part of the assessment procedure.

How to use this book

Depending on your experience you may not need every chapter in this book. Undergraduates are advised to quickly scan the whole book and get an overall impression of what dissertations are about. After reading it, go back to the beginning and start to work through it, chapter by chapter. When you actually begin your dissertation keep the book handy and use it as a guide.

Masters and Doctorate students may have already completed a dissertation on a previous course. Reflect back to those areas you found most challenging. Did it involve the choice of research methods, the evaluation of data, the collection and use of literature? Use the book to help with any problem areas.

Summary

Hopefully by now you will have a good idea of what dissertations are all about and the processes involved in producing one. The rest of the book gives more advice with respect to the different stages concerned.

The key points included in this chapter are:

- What is a dissertation?
- The role of dissertations on undergraduate and postgraduate courses.
- How this book can help you.

- The characteristic features of a dissertation.
- The academic, personal and career value of a dissertation.
- The stages involved in its production.
- The main skills you need to complete a dissertation.
- The role of supervisors.

2 Choosing and developing a subject to investigate

Introduction

This chapter starts to look at the mechanics of completing a dissertation. It will focus on two aspects: the choice of a topic to study, and how that topic may be refined and developed to form a framework for the dissertation. From the framework a proposal is then written which covers in more detail exactly what you want to do. Chapter 6 (page 85) describes how to write the proposal. From experience, the initial choice of subject often causes students a great deal of concern and seems to present a lot of problems. Depending on your degree programme the dissertation is possibly the most important piece of written work you undertake on your course. It is, therefore, essential to choose a subject that you can handle with confidence and interest. The correct choice of subject is the first step towards a successful dissertation.

In the early stages don't worry about the exact wording of a title as this can be decided later. The initial emphasis should be on selecting the general area and seeing if it is suitable, possibly using some of the techniques described below, to develop into a proposal.

This chapter considers a number of issues which are all inter-related. Don't consider each in isolation: always relate one to another to get the overall picture.

The issues discussed include:

- a discussion of the factors which may influence your choice;
- some of the things you can do to generate early ideas;
- a summary of the techniques you can try to establish the parameters of the dissertation.

Factors which may influence your choice of subject

There are a number of factors which may influence the choice of a dissertation topic. It may be either an outside interest or something connected with work. Read through the following, noting the points which apply to you.

- *Am I going to be genuinely interested in the topic?* A real interest in a subject is vitally important and helps when the going gets tough. At some stage it definitely will. Even with the brightest student, there comes a point when everything seems out of place and things don't go to plan. A genuine interest and commitment keeps you motivated; energy and enthusiasm are essential ingredients for a successful dissertation. To give an example, two students produced good dissertations by linking them with their outside interests. One student was keen on fashion and wrote on the role of 'modern designer labels' and the retail industry. The other, with a passion for football, researched the issue of 'football sponsorship' by large multinational companies.

- *Do I already know a lot about a topic?* You may already have a lot of information about a subject which could form the basis of a dissertation. For example, you may have collected a lot of material for a previous assignment which you never used. Why not use it now if you can?

- *Is it a well-trodden area?* Don't be afraid to choose a subject that is popular. For example, the management of change, governments and control of the banking sector, and e-business are current business issues. This means there is a great deal of information available. A lot of information does mean, however, that when searching through material you need to be really focused. Know exactly the sort of thing you are looking for. You must also make your treatment of the topic different – don't simply repeat a piece of research unless there are good and valid reasons.

- *Can I cope with the topic in terms of depth and breadth?* Dissertations must demonstrate appropriate academic rigour and depth: for example, some topics may need quantitative methods which could require a good level of mathematical ability. It is important to match the topic with your proven academic strengths and skills, so if quantitative methods and statistics are a real problem, choose an area that does not require advanced mathematical skills. Or at least be able and ready to develop specific skills for a particular method. An obvious example again is readiness to use statistics at the stage of data analysis. At doctoral level, you need to presume this is a prerequisite when developing your research topic. If you are good at talking to people and can empathize with their views, then go for the interview and similar techniques. There are, however, certain skills that all students need. These include effective information retrieval and writing skills.

- *Are the resources, e.g. time, facilities, money, equipment, etc. available?* It is important that any topic selected can be completed on time. Don't be over-ambitious; ensure that the final choice is feasible and manageable in the time available. Plan the work realistically, especially when deciding on the **methodology**. It takes time, for example, to run several focus groups, conduct **interviews** and record **observations**. Research costs money and with most dissertations, unless you are sponsored, it's the student who pays. You may decide to conduct a postal questionnaire, but can you afford the cost of postage? It may be possible to conduct the questionnaire by email. If you need to interview people, have you got the time and the money to do so? The resource factor should never be overlooked. With commercial research it is often finance which limits the type and scale of the final investigation. A useful exercise is to consider how your approach would change if there were unlimited resources available. This type of discussion often forms an interesting part of the discussion section of the final write up.

- *Availability of information.* Dissertations, especially at postgraduate level, need a lot of information. They require you to search out and assess the literature already published in the area. The literature has to be reviewed and this forms the background for your work. Literature is so important that a separate chapter is devoted to it (Chapter 7, page 106). Availability of published material should be a key factor when you make the final choice. Once an idea is identified, an initial literature search is essential. Be practical and realistic. If little or no material is easily retrieved you may be well advised to start again. Talk this through with your supervisor. A dissertation has to be completed within a fixed length of time. You haven't the luxury of an unlimited time span to work on a topic on which little has been published. Even with Doctorate degrees time seems to pass very quickly. Before you finally decide on a subject always double check that there is adequate information available.

- *Is the topic appropriate to my degree?* Business and management are academic subjects wide in scope. They cover almost anything 'from a pin to an elephant'. A pin company faces the same problems of finance, human resource management, marketing, operations, etc. as any other company. Elephants kept in zoos and nature reserves, which are run as independent organizations, face similar problems. You can give almost anything a business and management perspective. This provides enormous scope when selecting a topic to study. There is, however, a catch and, with certain topics, it is easy to lose the business and management focus. The following real-life examples will hopefully explain what can easily happen:

1. In earlier years UK farmers were encouraged to set aside part of their land for recreation and other non-agricultural purposes. The scheme when introduced was called 'set aside'. The dissertation's aim was to investigate the strategic management implications of the scheme. The student working on it became so interested in the way the land was used that the dissertation started to fit more closely with an environmental studies or agriculture degree.

2. A BA Business Studies student was interested to see if a proposed by-pass around St Helen's, Lancashire, UK would influence the economy of the town. The student became so engrossed with the planning and construction of the by-pass that the work was more relevant to a civil engineering and building degree.

3. This example concerns a student looking at management practices associated with factory farming. The student's focus wavered and the research became more concerned with ethical and animal rights issues. Although the work was good, it was not appropriate to a degree in Management Administration. With controversial topics like this, it is imperative that you keep a sense of balance. It is essential with academic work that any opinion, however contentious, is always based on evidence taken from either the literature or empirical research.

4. A student on a MBA Education Management degree looked at the management of a new reading programme being implemented at primary school level. The emphasis should have been on the implementation of the programme and how it was managed. The student became too interested in the pedagogical issues involved and whether the programme helped children to read. Although this should have been touched on briefly, it should not have been developed to any great extent; otherwise the dissertation would be more suited to an education degree.

5. Many contemporary business issues concern ethical opinions. For example, a student was interested in the marketing of GM foods. With this topic the emphasis must be placed on the marketing aspect. The student's work began to drift and concentrate more on the ethical implications concerning genetic engineering associated with GM foods. Although they would have a place in a dissertation on the marketing of GM foods, they must remain on the periphery of the work. The main focus must stay with marketing. If left unchecked, a final dissertation with this type of topic may be more appropriate to either a philosophy or sociology degree.

Fortunately, with all five students their supervisors picked up the loss of direction early on and excellent dissertations were produced. Always keep the main aim in mind and guard against veering off-track. It is essential that the dissertation's objectives relate in a very obvious way to your named degree.

- *Is the topic relevant to my needs?* Most students on any degree have some career idea in mind. Part-time students may already have a job and are often on a course to gain more qualifications to improve their career prospects. Why not, therefore, centre your dissertation on your present or future job? If you want to work in marketing, it makes sense to select a marketing topic. Use your dissertation to help build a CV and, as stated earlier, the completed work is something to take along to an interview. Even if it isn't finished it will at least give you something to talk about.

- *Does the topic agree with course regulations?* Always be aware of what you are supposed to produce. Certain courses set precise limits as to what can be done and the range of subjects that can be studied. Some degree programmes even give provisional titles. If you have any queries see your dissertation supervisor (see Chapter 1, page 11) and have a talk to resolve any issues. Follow their advice and use their experience.

Generating dissertation ideas – some things to do

So far we have worked through the factors that can influence your choice of subject, but you still need to choose the subject in the first place. The following may help you generate the initial idea.

- *Reading business and management literature.* Looking through new books and latest editions of journals may help. Recent publications reflect current trends and ideas on a subject; these are things which are happening now. There may be a number of subjects which you find interesting. Make a note of them, and using some of the techniques described in the next section, decide whether they can form the framework for a dissertation. From experience it is best to concentrate on articles found in journals. Journal titles vary from the general, e.g. *The Economist*, to the more specialized e.g. *Journal of Management Studies*. All are good and may help you come up with an idea. Also look up completed dissertations in your university library. Most keep a selection, especially at Masters and Doctorate level. See what earlier students have done – it often helps and gives you confidence that you can do the same.

- *I'd like to know more about that.* Has there been anything either on your current or previous course when you have thought to yourself 'That's interesting, I'd like to know more about that'? Often topics like this can be developed into a dissertation. Also you can re-use material collected for a previous assignment which you found especially interesting.

- *Current events and using the media e.g. TV, press, radio.* Events like big company takeovers often hit the headlines and similar current events can sometimes be used to develop good ideas. The government might announce new initiatives for industry which could become a starting point. In the world of business and management you must look out for, and be aware of, relevant contemporary issues. In the years 2012 and 2013 there was a lot of coverage about problems in the EU's Eurozone. Newspapers like the *Financial Times* report recent events and they can be a source of ideas. Many weekend papers have special business supplements that are worth looking through. There are many TV programmes on current affairs, business documentaries and business news. They may contain items that can form the basis of a dissertation.

- *Work experience.* Many undergraduate students, as part of their course, spend time away from the university in industry, on what is termed 'place-ment'. On some courses this can be as long as one year. Can this be the basis for starting a dissertation? You may be a part-time student and can use your job as a starting point for a dissertation, or you may have had a vacation job which can be used. In fact, any time spent in a commercial and external organization can often generate an idea. There may be a situation in the company that needs researching which can be the start of a dissertation. One example was a student working in a well-established and traditional family-run bleaching and dyeing company. The company was interested in investing in the introduction of new technology and equipment. This formed the basis for what turned out to be an excellent dissertation. Professional Doctorate students often work in areas that may generate their research topic. However, if you have contact with a company and would like to use them as a basis for a dissertation it is essential to obtain their written per-mission. When working in an organization you may see confidential informa-tion which the company wishes to remain unpublished. Although it may be good material to use in a dissertation, you cannot use it unless it is possible to keep the completed dissertation confidential. It would be wise to talk this through with your supervisor. A word of caution when using real-life exam-ples: companies often expect the student to produce a type of consultancy report. A dissertation and a consultancy report are not the same thing. A report pays more attention to final recommendations and outcomes, whereas the dissertation also requires the literature to be reviewed in detail and the methodology carefully worked out. Moreover, a dissertation relates academic theory and practice with respect to the topic being researched – again, this is usually absent in a consultancy report.

Developing the idea – some techniques to try

Selecting the general topic is only the start. It now needs to be refined and developed in order to determine if it can be expanded into a dissertation. You are going to take your original idea and see how it may be broken down into smaller, discrete areas. These can then be rearranged and structured into a logical sequence to form the framework of the dissertation. In other words, you have to draw up an initial dissertation outline that will form the basis for the proposal (Chapter 6, page 85).

However, don't be too ambitious – you only have a limited amount of time to complete a dissertation. It's not going to be your life's work. A criticism levelled by many external examiners, especially with undergraduate dissertations, is that they are too wide and unfocused; they lack direction. It is far better to study a small topic in considerable detail than attempt a broad subject which, because of its complexity, only allows a superficial level of analysis.

At this early stage you are trying to generate a series of **research questions** (sometimes called research objectives). Ask yourself, for each area identified, questions like 'What do I want to find out?', 'Which research methods would be the best to use?', and 'How can this topic be investigated and researched?'

In summary, take your early idea and divide it up into smaller ideas. Look at each small idea in turn and decide if it's worth keeping. If it is, then decide on the best method(s) to use to research it, in order to make it part of a larger piece of work. You are trying to determine the precise focus of the study and a list of the ideas, together with the ways in which you intend to research them.

At this early stage carry out an initial literature search to identify how much information is available. At the start there isn't time to read everything you find, but keep a full record of all items you discover. Attempt to trace about ten recent review articles. Together they should provide the current state of knowledge on the subject. These should give enough background on which to base the dissertation. Once the dissertation is in full swing, then the full literature search can begin.

If this early search identifies only a very small number of references, seriously consider abandoning the original topic and starting again. You must have a fair amount of published work from which to start so you can review the literature, and relate your research to established theory on the subject. As stated earlier, availability of information is a key factor in determining the success of a dissertation. If relevant literature is hard to find then discuss the problem with your supervisor and follow their advice.

Established researchers have experience to fall back on to help them to take an initial idea and build it into a structured outline. If you are uncertain how to go about this, then a number of techniques can be used to develop the initial idea. These are described below. Give all of them a try and see which you prefer. Each one helps you produce a 'shopping list' of things to look for when you continue your literature search. During these early stages give some thought to drawing up a provisional timetable. Estimate how much time you think each part may take. It is very easy to spend too much time on one area and then have to rush the writing up at the end.

Here are some basic techniques to help you develop your initial idea.

- *Mind mapping.* This is an excellent way to come up with original ideas and is popular in business. It is also referred to as concept or thought mapping, and is often used in groups in staff development and training workshops. The first edition of this book started out as a mind map. Start with a large sheet of paper, and if you have big handwriting, A3 (420 × 297mm) size is good. Write the main idea in the middle of the paper and then write down around the title, like the spokes of a wheel, anything that comes to mind about the topic. You can work in a clockwise or anti-clockwise direction. It doesn't matter. Don't worry if any of the subjects appear out of place, they can be deleted later. You are trying to generate as many ideas as possible about your early dissertation idea. Some students find it easier to use coloured pens. When you run out of ideas go back and review each one in turn, crossing out those which you feel are unsuitable. It is also helpful to think how you would go about researching each one. When the remaining ideas are finally arranged in a logical order you normally have a good outline for a dissertation. Figure 2.1 shows a mind map for a dissertation on online shopping and the retail industry. This technique helps you think creatively, and is sometimes referred to as a non-linear technique. The advantage of this type of approach is that on one sheet of paper you get an overview of all the ideas on one particular subject in one place. For techniques like mind mapping software packages are now available.
- *The sticky pad technique.* This method uses a pad of 'Post-it' or similar self-adhesive notes. If you prefer, you can use small sheets of either card or paper. It's like mind mapping in that you write down all the ideas which come to mind – one idea on each sheet of paper. At the end spread all the pieces in front of you and arrange them in a logical order, rejecting those that seem out of place. The advantage over mind mapping is that as you move

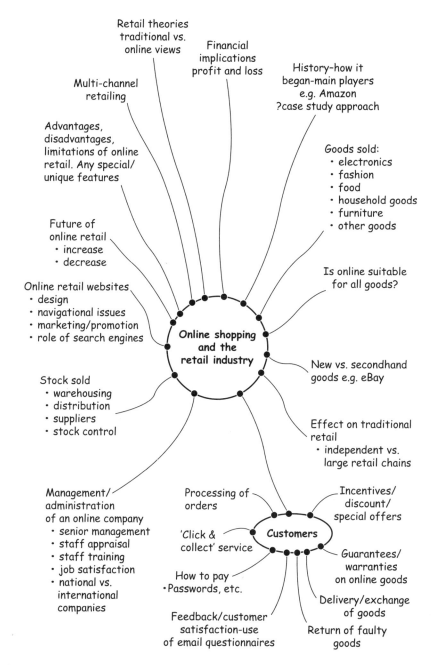

Figure 2.1 Mind map for the dissertation 'An investigation into the impact of online shopping on the retail industry'

the papers around you spark off new thoughts and suggestions, and these can be added to the pile of notes. Finally, copy onto a fresh sheet of paper your final list of research objectives. Some researchers call this method '**cluster analysis**'. Don't confuse it with the statistical term '**cluster sampling**'; the two are not the same.

- *Question time approach.* Often the above techniques become untidy and messy. Some students prefer to work in a neater fashion and write things down in lists. This can be done by asking simple straightforward questions. They may be enough to trigger the imagination. Questions like Who?, What?, Where?, When?, How?, and Why? will suffice. Make the questions as focused as possible and decide exactly what you want to find out. Ask questions about the type of information needed and the best research methods to use to investigate each idea identified.

- *Concepts, trends, implications and issues.* This is very much like the question time approach, but you start with a series of general questions such as: Are there any economic concepts, trends, implications and issues involved? Are there any technological concepts, trends, implications and issues involved? Are there any legal concepts, trends, implications and issues involved? Are there any social concepts, trends, implications and issues involved? From these general questions you can delve more deeply and again come up with a number of more focused issues on your original idea.

In addition to the above, a number of other techniques are available, e.g. **fish bone diagrams**, flow charts and **relevance trees** that work just as well. All of them are simple and, when used correctly, can be very effective. You can use each one singly or in combination to suit your way of working. Always use a method that best suits you and your dissertation.

The next step is to expand these early thoughts into a fully detailed **research proposal** and this is described in Chapter 6 (page 85). This involves deciding on the best methodological approaches to use and selecting suitable data collection techniques. These are considered in the following chapters.

Summary

This chapter has looked at the start of the dissertation process. It has focused on the identification of an idea and how that can be developed to form a suitable dissertation subject. This is summarized in Figure 2.2.

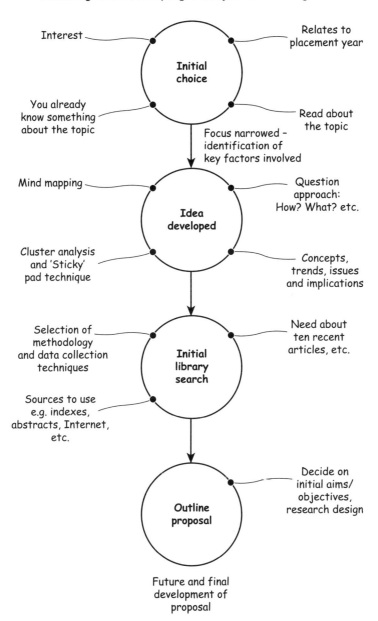

Figure 2.2 A suggested scheme to develop a dissertation topic

The key points included in the chapter are:

- Factors which may influence your choice of subject.
- Some things to do to generate a dissertation idea.
- Some techniques to try to develop the initial idea.
- The importance of a clearly stated purpose in the research.

3 Doing your research: design, methodology and method

Introduction

So far we have explained what is meant by the term 'dissertation' and the key things you need to think about when starting one. Advice has been given about choosing and developing a suitable topic to study. Mention has been made of the importance of research and the practical considerations that need to be borne in mind. Care also needs to be taken, however, not only in choosing a topic to study, but in deciding how to study it. Working out a **research design** or plan is a good start. The selection of an appropriate **methodology** and the choice of suitable techniques are of paramount importance.

This chapter considers some basic ideas that help shape your approach to doing research and your research design. These include what is meant by research and how this relates to business and management, whether particular methodological approaches are more suitable and reliable than others, and how these ideas lead to a selection of appropriate methods for the research. There is always a range of possible methods from which you can choose. These deliberations reflect a crucial time in thinking about your project, so share your ideas with your supervisor. The importance of your research design should be discussed, perhaps several times, with a consideration of the following issues:

- What do you want to know? Make a statement of your purpose (i.e. your **research intention**).
- What is it you need to understand? Identify the nature and context(s) for the information or evidence you plan to gather.
- Where or how will you access this knowledge? Be sure about why and who it will involve.
- Are there any ethical issues and how do you retain integrity in the research design? Ensure the research is safe, sound and will do no harm?

A key skill relevant to good research is critical reflection. This means you revisit the fundamental purpose of the research in a reflexive way and think about your research intention. A process of reflexion should run continuously throughout the dissertation. This means building points of reflexion in all stages of the dissertation. It can be referred to within the written dissertation, for example, in the research plan, during data collection (and during any pilot research) and post data collection. A reflexive summary statement can be included towards the end of the dissertation such as in the conclusion, dependent upon the dissertation regulations of your university. The use of literature is an important part of this process. Ask yourself what are you trying to achieve, find out, know more about and how will you manage this project? In turn, a key task at this stage of planning is always aim to ensure 'do-ability'. In other words, can your dissertation be completed on time in the time available? Resource constraints, deadlines, distances between place and space in which research activity is sited, and scheduling time with work–life balance are just some of the factors you need to manage.

Although common sense tells us, quite correctly, that doing a dissertation is a developmental task with a start and a finish, you will find that the process is less straightforward. It is iterative. It involves you in moving forward but at different points in time returning to think about or reflect on earlier parts of the research project. A good example of this is how you consider ethics as a part of this process. The temptation is to do this as a 'one off' before engaging with fieldwork. It is much better to think about ethics as a continuing consideration throughout the entire process of producing a dissertation. The overall movement in this process is one of coalescence as different parts of the design come together and this brings with it a satisfaction for a well-worked plan. The following discussion looks at the main steps in constructing and following this research plan.

Research design

Research design is a general term that covers a number of separate, but related, issues associated with research. It includes the aims of the research, the final selection of the appropriate methodology, the data collection techniques you intend to use, the chosen methods of data analysis and interpretation, and how all this fits in with the literature. Figure 3.1 attempts to link all these issues together as an illustration of the research process.

Two important concepts to build into research design are **validity** or creditability and **reliability** or trustworthiness. Validity is concerned with the idea that the research design fully addresses the research questions and objectives you are trying to answer and achieve, and the findings reflect appropriately collected and correctly analyzed data. This implies that as much planning as possible must

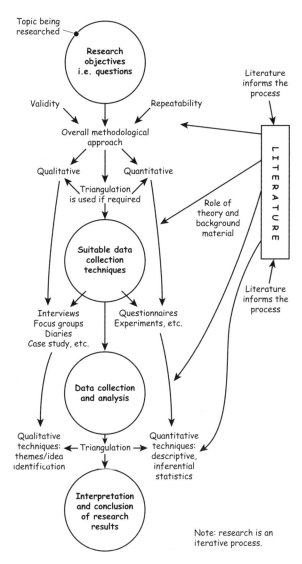

Figure 3.1 A summary of the features of research design

be done beforehand. Reliability is about consistency, veracity and credibility. It is in part tied to the idea of replication and whether another researcher could use your design and obtain similar findings. This does not imply that their interpretation and conclusions will be the same. The chances are that they will be different, since this is where the judgement of individual researchers comes into play. Overall, the research design is the blueprint or detailed outline for the whole of your research and dissertation. It relies on careful forward planning.

Methodology and methods

The approach a researcher uses to investigate a subject is termed the *methodology*. Methodology aligns to the philosophical basis on which the research is founded. The particular techniques used to collect data and information are termed *methods*. Don't become confused by the terms 'methodology' and 'method' – the two are not the same but are closely related. Methodology is the research **rationale** and conceptual framework for your research design. When you consider research methodology, you may well refer to research methods but you should at this point in your work focus upon the logic behind using these methods in the context of your research. The scientific tradition encourages the researcher to explain in any account of their research methodology why they are using a particular method or technique so that research results are capable of being evaluated. Research methods are the range of techniques, tools and/or procedures that are used to generate and collect data. For example, an **interview** can be called a research instrument or tool, but interviewing is a research technique and will involve a particular procedure.

Although there are many established ways of approaching a problem and collecting material, do not be afraid to try new ways of research. You must, of course, provide a thorough and well thought out rationale to back up any new idea. This rationale and approach is your own research methodology. Explaining this methodology is a key part to any dissertation. It is widely regarded by examiners as a strong indicator of the scholarly value and quality found in a dissertation. A weak dissertation will often include an obligatory description of methodology, rehearsing some of the features associated with either a quantitative or qualitative paradigm. A 'paradigm' is a set of assumptions, concepts, values and practices that constitutes a way of viewing reality for the community that shares them, especially in an intellectual discipline. In social science research, two major paradigms associated with research are the quantitative paradigm and the qualitative paradigm.

What is invariably missing when a student considers the place of paradigm in their research is using this knowledge to explain the nature and approach to the research as a rationale. You should use it as a basis for the research design. Before reading what comes next, reflect upon key terms new to you in this section. You will see if you skim forward that some of the key terms are more fully considered. Track back and see how each term can be applied to your dissertation topic.

What is research?

Before the different approaches and techniques are explained, it is important to address a very basic question. What is research? Academics who study the philosophy of research consider this question at some length and in some detail.

This is not the intention here; the aim is to give you a basic understanding so that you think seriously about how you intend to investigate your selected topic. It is useful, whether you are an undergraduate or postgraduate, and if you wish you extend and add to your knowledge as a researcher, that you explore the meaning and implications of three key philosophical terms for your research. Each plays its part, regardless of whether you are aware of this, in shaping the kind of research you conduct. These key philosophical terms are:

- Ontology. This is concerned with the nature of existence. It is bound up with a particular belief in what exists, or theory about the nature of being, or the kinds of things that have existence. The implications for research are bound up with decisions about the place or relevance of ideas associated with validity, reliability, subjectivity, objectivity and truth.
- Epistemology. This is the study of knowledge and justified belief. It serves as the basis for knowledge, and types of evidence, information and the way we interpret and construct our findings for a piece of research. Ideas about methodology and method are, for example, shaped by epistemic principles adopted by the researcher. Similarly, epistemic issues arise when working on the creation and different forms of dissemination of knowledge in particular areas of inquiry.
- Axiology. This is the study of value, or goodness, in its widest sense. It plays a constant part in decisions and conduct in research design. A simple example of this role is in the adoption of ethical principles. It also reflects much more wide-ranging issues to do with the on-going relationships between the researcher, research participants, and the research itself.

A useful source for greater discussion of these terms and methodology and how each affects research design in business and management is Johnson and Duberley (2000).

Different academics define research in different ways. A useful starting point when thinking about research is offered by Bassey (1999). He writes that, 'Research is systematic, critical and self-critical enquiry which aims to contribute to the advancement of knowledge and wisdom.' Another easy-to-understand explanation is that given by Creswell (2008). He defines research as '... a process of steps used to collect and analyze information to increase our understanding of a topic or issue.' This process consists of three traditional steps:

1. ask a question;
2. find data with which to answer the question;
3. report an answer to the question.

Johnson (1994) highlights the following four key suggestions in a similar approach to research:

1. **Research should be focused, not general.** For example, if you were investigating the role of *Adaptive Leadership* (AL) and its importance for industry, would it be better to look at all industries (e.g. marketing, leisure, manufacturing, etc.), or one in great detail? This means that when you begin a piece of research you need to set up precise research questions to decide exactly what you want to do.

2. **Research needs to be systematic – the approach to a problem should be structured and organized.** Take the above example with respect to a particular manufacturing company. Would you ask every employee you came across in the company what they thought about AL or would it be better first to think about the issues associated with AL and arrive at a series of structured questions? You could then put the same set of questions to a selected number of people in the company. To arrive at the questions you would need to find out what other people had written about AL and how this may be related to manufacturing. This would involve collecting information already available. You would then collect and evaluate your own data and compare it with existing material. This would be a synthesis of the new material with the old, forming a new set of knowledge.

3. **Research entails moving beyond generally available knowledge.** Carrying out research implies that you add to present knowledge. After completing the work on AL you should know more about the concept and have a greater insight into its issues and problems. This in turn may generate more research ideas that need to be resolved and studied further.

4. **A basis for analysis and elucidatory comments.** After having carried out research you should be able to arrive at some conclusions that may agree or disagree with current accepted theory and understanding about AL and the manufacturing industry. Either way, you would need to provide a reasoned account to support your case. If your work were limited to one manufacturing company, you would need to consider how your results related to the manufacturing industry as a whole. It may even be possible to make tentative conclusions about the implications and potential impact of AL and all industry. If you want to know more about AL, an overview in the book written by Heifetz, Linsky and Grashow (2009) is a good start.

In summary, research involves finding out about things, but in a structured way. If you were about to buy a new computer, smart-phone, hi-fi, or even a house, you would look around, compare prices, after-sales service, and so on. You might look at specialist magazines, watch a consumer programme on TV, etc. In other words, before you bought anything you would collect evidence and evaluate it before making a final decision. The same procedure applies to the research involved in writing a dissertation.

Research and business practice

The research context is without question the primary consideration for the student preparing a **research proposal**. This does not just mean the place in which to carry out fieldwork. It is also the intellectual context. It is essential to relate how the meaning of research applies to the world of business, and if there is anything special about it. Easterby-Smith, Thorpe and Jackson (2012), for example, regard management research as distinctive. They argue it is eclectic, i.e. wide-ranging, and crosses many subject boundaries. It is, therefore, difficult to centre research in one particular discipline. Business and management research (BMR) is by its nature an applied research with an overriding interest in utility and impact.

The general purpose of the research in your dissertation will be tied to securing a high level of relevance and ideally impact upon the field in which the research has been completed. This is often characterized as being in some way significant and reflecting a contribution of originality or new knowledge. For example, has your research extended the knowledge base of the subject, caused a significant change in a real place of work, or influenced in some way the professional practice of the people involved in the research?

Similarly, Hodgkinson (2001) describes BMR as a 'problematic problem field' that is largely distinctive because of its eclectic nature and subject matter. Student-led research in business and management, nonetheless, remains an activity located in a multi-subject, multi-disciplinary field in which a wide range of research strategies can be applied. This in turn means research in this field needs to develop collaborative skills as well as subject-specific technical skills and cultural aware-ness, even though the research methodology remains the same as that for the rest of the social sciences.

Invariably, as a consequence of research, business and management profes-sional practice is often changed and improved. Research is not always carried out for research's sake. In a discipline such as chemistry, research, although important, often simply adds to the body of knowledge of the subject. The research itself, unless it results in new techniques, does not always bring about any change in the way chemists work. In management, however, the results of research often change the way managers act and carry out their daily work. Imagine research has been car-ried out into the way senior executives greet their staff first thing in the morning, and it was found that a handshake improved productivity and profits. The chances are that all executives would make the point of shaking the hands of their employees as often as possible. The behaviour of the executives, therefore, would have been influenced by the research. This example is somewhat simple, but in business and management, research is often related to professional practice.

Senior managers and executives are powerful people and usually difficult to contact. They have influence over their employees' lives in terms of job security, pay and conditions. The researcher may face problems gaining access to executives. If access is achieved, and the research completed, what happens if the findings are controversial? Business research can put the researcher in a vulnerable position, especially if they are part of the company being researched. This issue of 'insider research' is more fully discussed later in the book as it is often the case that a student engaged in part-time study will research their own organization.

Finally, all organizations deal with confidential and commercial issues. Access to these by the researcher may be difficult and, if it is allowed, it might not be possible to publish the research in the public domain. There are ethical issues here, which depending on the topic, may compromise the researcher and other people concerned. This again makes research in business and management somewhat different.

The research process

Business and management research is a process, a series of activities unfolding over time. It involves a number of things such as choice of the research design, the collection of data, the evaluation of results, and so on. It also requires the student to establish and manage two important relationships. The first is with their dissertation supervisor as previously explained. The second is more abstract and is relevant at this point when considering the interaction between research process and design. It is what we have called the 'research relationship' (see Figure 3.2). It involves three prime elements: the first is the researcher who is the prime mover in the relationship; the second is the research participant (be it individual, group or community) that interacts with the researcher; the third is the research itself.

The successful management of this relationship involves use of time, place and space reflecting consent, assent and on-going interaction between each and all of the three elements in the research design, as well as a developmental process. It is a movement that reflects both a series of structures established in the design of the research, and the agency of various participants in the research process.

One of the most important decisions to make, as previously explained, is the general approach the research is going to take. There are different schools of

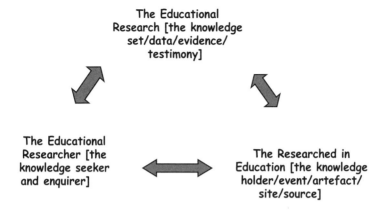

The Educational
Research [the knowledge
set/data/evidence/
testimony]

The Educational
Researcher [the
knowledge seeker
and enquirer]

The Researched in
Education [the knowledge
holder/event/artefact/
site/source]

Figure 3.2 The research relationship in the research design

thought on this. As identified above, academics spend a great deal of time discussing the philosophy of research and research design. A lengthy account here is unnecessary, but a basic understanding will help to clarify your choice of methodology and research design. It will help you decide which approach is best in a particular situation, and how this will help form the particular features of the research relationship. It will assist if you need either to create a new methodology, or modify an existing one, as may happen.

A criticism made by many examiners about dissertations is that the research methodology lacks clarity and direction. In many instances the method of data collection is not well thought out or suitable to the subject being investigated. Often at the early stages students become impatient and simply want to chase results and information. Remember, how you collect evidence is as important as the evidence itself. If your results are to be believed, then the way you collect them in the first place must also be plausible, trustworthy and credible.

The idea of methodological fit is described by Edmondson and McManus (2007) as a way of categorizing knowledge generated by three types of management research (nascent, mature and intermediate). Research design is shaped by the kind of knowledge you want to generate and should play a big part in thinking about the research intention:

- Nascent knowledge is made up of explanations or tentative connections between phenomena and is associated with original approaches to research in which novel questions of 'how' and 'why' are asked.
- Mature knowledge comprises well-developed theory associated with research, reinforcing fully established models and constructs accepted in a discipline and research community.

- Intermediate knowledge is a mix of mature and nascent, and associated with the development of testable hypotheses, similar to mature theory research, or with open-ended research questions exploring constructs that remain at best tentative, similar to nascent theory research.

Thinking about this best fit in research design also means considering which methodological paradigms support your research intention. These paradigms are most frequently a mix of three: qualitative, quantitative, or hybrid mixed methods methodology. The idea of 'methodological fit' builds on methodological guidelines found more generally in the literature and in turn helps with construction of design and the choice of techniques, tools and forms of analysis and report.

Taking this idea of fitness of purpose further, we can think about some of the basic methodological choices, noting that each approach has different advantages and limitations. The ultimate test for each point in the process is how well or poorly a selection will serve to achieve the stated research intention with respect to your dissertation.

Methodology is also concerned with how the researcher views the world in which he or she carries out the research. Suppose you are a member of a group, and are researching how that group reacts in different situations. It could be argued that as a group member, it would be very difficult to stand back and be truly impartial, or indeed not influence either the way you study the group's activity or the group's relationship with you. On the other hand, it could be argued that, with suitable techniques, it is possible to stand back and take a more objective view on how to research the group.

In the main, therefore, academics traditionally distinguish two main kinds of research, or more accurately, research paradigms: *quantitative* and *qualitative* research. Quantitative research involves an objective way of studying things, whereas a qualitative approach assumes that this is difficult and the research is subjective.

The quantitative research paradigm: sometimes referred to as *positivist,* is also perceived widely as scientific in approach. It aims to be objective and collects and uses **numerical data**. Such research is associated with experimental design, the study of causal effect and a belief that research conditions can be controlled and manipulated so as to produce generalizable results or facts about the phenomenon studied. In this type of research, data or results are given numerical values and the researcher uses a mathematical and statistical treatment to help evaluate the results. Scientists carrying out experiments use this approach. **Surveys** by marketing people, using **questionnaires** and **interviews** where responses are given numerical values, would also be described as quantitative research. In quantitative research, methods are frequently employed to establish general laws or principles based upon measurement. This scientific approach is often labelled *nomothetic* – it assumes social reality is objective and external to the individual and we are a part of a fixed universe.

The qualitative research paradigm: this is based on a view that it is not desirable or preferred for researchers to stand back and be objective, since they are really part of the process being researched. This type of research may be termed *relativist, constructivist* or *phenomenological.* The data collected in qualitative research is often descriptions and is sometimes described as 'rich' or 'contextualized', emphasizing the importance of the research site. It places even greater weight upon the ways in which the research relationship and process interact to produce data, as well as interaction between the researcher and the data in what is sometimes called an 'interpretative paradigm'. According to Cresswell (1994), a qualitative study is '… an inquiry process of understanding a social or human problem, based on building a complex, holistic picture, formed with words, reporting detailed views of informants, and conducted in a natural setting.' The naturalistic approach to research emphasizes the importance of the subjective experience and belief in a social reality, and is labelled idiographic. A prime purpose in this research is reaching an understanding of the meaning of phenomena and often involves an evaluation of events seen as a personal and subjective construction (Burns, 2000).

Academics argue about the merits and limitations of each approach and, sometimes, even what each term really means. It is easier at this point to see that the assumptions about research that underpin these decisions and even the forming of these and other research paradigms, are ontological and epistemological in nature, although these assumptions are often taken for granted.

As far as your dissertation is concerned, the advice is always to adopt the methodology that best suits your background, interest and, most importantly, the subject you are investigating. Try to get a 'methodological fit' and sustain this in the construction and implementation of your research design. The various research tools and techniques of data collection associated with each approach are described in Chapters 4 and 5.

Mixed methods methodology: can you combine qualitative and quantitative research?

Yes. It is easy to see that trying to ensure methodological fit means very often constructing a research design that will need a mix of approaches. A weak dissertation can be the result of a student wishing to specifically avoid managing a nomothetic or idiographic form of analysis and method. This can often lead to mismatch between the method and research intention in the design of the research project. On the other hand, a mix of methods may reflect an unfolding design: you might, for example, decide to carry out a survey after investigating a subject from a qualitative perspective. For example, after studying certain changes in an organization, you may decide to survey, by questionnaire, opinions (e.g. those of managers, administrative staff, clients, etc.) about a particular aspect associated with the change.

For these reasons, and a general dissatisfaction amongst researchers with experiencing an 'either or' approach to using qualitative and quantitative research, which has been dubbed the era of the 'paradigm wars', a hybrid form of research paradigm called 'mixed methods methodology' (MMM) has emerged. Mixed methods research involves collecting, analyzing and mixing qualitative and quantitative approaches at many phases in the research design and process. As a method, it focuses on collecting, analyzing, and mixing quantitative and qualitative data in a single study or series of studies as a combination. It is important as an approach and sometimes can better meet the complexity of topic(s) being studied. If you want to know more about MMM, Tashakkori and Teddlie (2010) is a good start.

Ethical considerations and research: from start to finish

It may help to start by explaining more clearly what is meant by ethics. As you can imagine, many academics have written a great deal about it, and one of the most straightforward definitions of ethics is that of Churchill (1995): 'moral principles and values that govern the way an individual or group conducts its activities'.

Business research comes into direct contact with people either individually, or when they are part of a larger group, such as in a company or an organization. Moreover, much of the research is qualitative in approach, and the outcome of the research can be subject to wide interpretation. As such, the **biases**, intent and views of everyone concerned with a piece of research are open to influence, change and debate. There are occasions, therefore, when the researcher (in this case, you) needs an appreciation of the ethical issues that may be involved at all stages of the research.

Nowadays universities pay particular attention to ethical and associated issues and have codes of practice, protocols and procedures that both staff and students are expected to follow. Most universities have an ethics committee or something similar that produces guidelines as well as proformas used to monitor and approve research activity. This includes all research of both staff and students including that conducted by students carrying out a dissertation. A number of professional bodies (e.g. the British Sociological Association) also produce guidelines with respect to the conduct of research. As a researcher it is your responsibility to ensure that you follow any prescribed codes where they are applicable.

In addition to this requirement on the ethical aspects included in your work, we would say more generally, that good conduct requires a student in their research to observe the following 'rules' or principles in their work:

- Only involve people with their consent or knowledge. Participants should always have enough information about the research to make an informed decision as to whether to take part or not. During the research participants should retain the right to draw back and remove consent if they so wish.
- Never coerce or persuade people to participate in research. Participants have the right to choose for themselves whether to be the subject of your research.
- Never withhold information on the true nature of the research. Explain to all concerned what it's all about.
- Tell the truth about the research and never deceive participants in any way.
- Never induce participants to do things that could destroy their self-confidence or self-determination.
- Never expose people to situations that could cause mental or physical stress.
- Always respect a participant's right to privacy. If anonymity (total protection from any identification of the individual or breach of privacy) and confidentiality (all data is kept safe, secure and will not be reported in a form that can be attributed to the individual research participant) are guaranteed, this should always be maintained.
- Treat all groups in the same research project alike, with consideration and respect.

Finally, when you write up your research, you should present the evidence with honesty and integrity and never knowingly allow anyone to misuse or misinterpret your work. People who have taken part in the research also have a right to know about the results of the research, unless there are very valid reasons to the contrary.

Summary

This chapter has presented some very basic ideas to help shape your approach to doing research and your research design.

The key points included in this chapter are:

- Maintaining a good working relationship with your dissertation supervisor(s).
- Preparing a summary outline of the research design or proposal as a working blueprint or plan for your study.
- Thinking about methodological fit and understanding the inter-relationship between methodology and method.
- Raising your own awareness and understanding of the assumptions underpinning BMR, including how aspects of philosophical knowledge shape the rationale and approach to research.
- Reflecting upon the iterative nature of the research process and how to manage the fitting together of separate parts of the research design, process and task at the same time.
- Anticipate how you will manage the three key elements of the research relationship to allow you to successfully organize and complete your dissertation.
- The importance of ethical considerations with respect to research.

4   The qualitative paradigm: tools, techniques and tips

Introduction

The previous chapter explained what is meant by research and how to approach its design as part of a dissertation project. We briefly discussed the differences between mixed, qualitative and quantitative methodology in research. This chapter focuses specifically on how the qualitative paradigm impacts upon research. The examples of **case study** and action research are used to show how a research design can require either a mixed methodology or be entirely located within the qualitative paradigm. The purpose of the research (i.e. the **research intention**) should always determine the methodology used and the choice of any qualitative methods adopted in the final design. Some qualitative data collection tools and techniques are explained, and how to approach data analysis and ways to report the findings are considered. Finally, some tips on how to best work through this stage of the research process are given.

Qualitative research is a staple form of research in the social sciences, politics and economics, all subjects closely linked with business. It is a descriptive, non-numerical way to collect and interpret information, and is sometimes called an **'idiographic'** methodology. Researchers who adopt this approach argue that no two situations are the same and every phenomenon is unique. The research data cannot, therefore, be measured in the experimental sense, since it takes place in actual and everyday settings, not in a laboratory. It investigates the way people react, work, live and manage their daily lives.

The researcher in a qualitative paradigm is identified as a substantial part of the research being carried out. This further complicates the situation. For example, a student carrying out an in-house dissertation on some aspect of a company is part of that company. It could be claimed that the student is too involved to stand back and be truly objective (i.e. adopt a positivist paradigm). With a qualitative investigation the researcher observes a great deal and any results are mostly descriptive in nature rather than sets of numerical data. Over the years a number of different qualitative tools and techniques have evolved. Some of the more widely used techniques are explained in this chapter. These include using research tools such as **interviews**, **observation** and the use of **diaries**.

It may seem a trivial point, but it is important to remember that a 'research method' is a way of describing the practical work carried out in a research enquiry. This involves a combination of procedures, techniques and report. It is easy to confuse method with methodology. A case study or action research are examples of methodology. Another way of putting this is to think of case studies or action research as a research approach, involving a particular strategy and, each in turn, employs a number of different methods and tools (sometimes quantitative ones). In the main, however, these approaches seek more descriptive information, both in the collection and interpretation of data. This is because the research intention associated, for example, with action research is located in a practical setting. It focuses upon a particular set of issues in a specific 'real world' context.

The description of some main methods which follow is not definitive and the annotated bibliography should help if you need more information. Whether you adopt a mixed, qualitative or quantitative methodology, remember you are not expected to use every technique going. What is essential is that the final choice is relevant to, and workable, with your particular topic. Moreover, be aware of the advantages and limitations involved and repeatedly revisit the **rationale** for the final selection. The reasoning behind the choice is never wasted, as it can and should be written up and included in the methodology section of the final dissertation.

Case studies

As highlighted previously, a case study is not a single qualitative technique, since a number of methods are used. It is easy to confuse a case study with case examples, or more often termed **vignettes**. A vignette is a device for illustrating an aspect of testimony or other specific data. Finch (1987) describes vignettes as '*short stories about hypothetical characters in specified circumstances, to whose situation the interviewee is invited to respond*'. Many recent Government documents include the use of vignettes (often casually called case studies). They are used to either illustrate 'best practice' and/or to infer evidence-based support for policy development and guidance. Vignettes, owing to time constraints, are unlikely to be used in undergraduate work, but can be used with great effect in postgraduate dissertations. Note also that case studies may not be only qualitative in nature. Many include quantitative questionnaires, although they tend to make more use of descriptive evidence such as interviews and observation.

A case study may be defined as an extensive study of a single situation such as an individual, family or organization. Johnson (1994) defines a case study as,

'*An enquiry which uses multiple sources of evidence. It investigates a contemporary phenomenon within its real life context when the boundaries between phenomenon and context are not clearly evident.*' Kenyan (2009) provides one recent and relevant example of an analytic case study. The collective memory, that is, the recollection of what has been experienced in common by a discrete group, was explored by researching a selected group of CEOs in Israel. Collective memory is identified as a powerful force in an organization that when harnessed is used to consolidate cohesion within a group, or across the divide between different groups in times of conflict. A second alternative and interesting example of the case study as an idea and a tool in 'market branding' and 'product placement' can be found at: http://blogs.hbr.org/cs/2013/01/treat_everything_as_a_case _study.html.

Plant (2013) describes a reflexive insight into the powerful versatility of the 'case study' while driving down the highway on the first stage of a vacation. He asks if it might really be useful to apply case study to a wide range of business management operations. The title to the blog is 'treat everything as a case study'!

A dissertation example using a case study approach might be to study the introduction of a new IT system into a company. The research would look at the company before and after the introduction. The benefits and limitations of the system would be assessed. The effects on the workforce, management and clients could also be considered. A case study is, in reality, a detailed example investigated from multiple perspectives. Case studies are popular and excellent in situations that are complex, involving a number of different issues. Case studies can be used in all aspects of management, but are generally used as a 'problem-solving' exercise which involves a 'puzzle' that needs a solution, or as an 'analytic' explanatory exercise to try to understand wider or more theoretical issues, by asking what happened and why. With case studies it is not always necessary to identify problems or suggest solutions, but it is imperative to clearly state the research purpose at the start.

Types of case study

All case studies are inductive in that they report on the particular and specific, and then try to relate that to the general picture. They can be used as we have previously suggested either to generate theory and ideas about a topic, or to test out a theory to see if it occurs and applies in a real life situation.

There are different forms of case study. They may be described as follows:

- **Typical.** Here the organization studied is as typical as possible, for example, a large supermarket or general manufacturing company. The IT example above would fall into this category. Many companies over recent years have taken on and introduced new technology and there is a lot of literature on the subject. This type of research is often used to test and examine accepted ideas on a subject.

- **Atypical.** Here the example is usually an out of the ordinary event. It is a 'one off' – it does not happen every day. The research is used to explore the breakdown of a business project. For example, as with the case study of the Google-China debacle. There is an ongoing dispute linked to agreed part-nership and collaboration with online development in China (Grogan and Brett, 2006). Case studies like this add to knowledge and may initiate the development of new theories and ideas about a subject. In this instance, it may impact upon global attitudes and practice related to online access and the principle of '*net neutrality*' in the business of using the Internet.
- **Precursor studies.** With large research projects case studies are sometimes used at the start and act as precursors to identify the issues involved before the final research is planned in detail.
- **Multiple case studies.** If time is available it is a good idea to study two or more similar examples. This allows for a comparative treatment and, as a result, helps build and confirm accepted theory.

The main question you need to answer is why you have chosen a case study approach in the first place. This may come down to cost, time or accessibility (especially if you work in the organization). These are valid reasons and need documenting in the final write up of a dissertation.

The importance of context and background

As a case study tends to look at one example, it is essential that its context and background are described and explained in order to provide a full picture of the situation under investigation. With case study research, because of its unique-ness, it is important to 'set the scene' for the reader. This gives the research credibility and makes it academically more valid.

The contextual features to note with a case study include:

- the history and location of the organization: how it has developed over time to its current position;
- details of any similar case study research to help in the comparison of ideas and theory;
- an account of the national and possibly international picture. If you were working with a small building firm, some working knowledge of how the local building industry is organized may provide relevant background material;
- the current management structure of the organization being studied and how it works on a 'day-to-day' basis;

- the role and influence of government and other institutions (both local and central). Changes in law, tax rules, etc. all affect business and these may have a bearing on the case in question;
- the role of currently accepted theory. If you were looking at motivation in a company you would need to review the theories of motivation against what was actually happening in the company.

An important feature to watch out for when describing the context and background of a case study is that you do not take it too far. For instance, if you were investigating the marketing strategy of a company you would obviously need to look at the suppliers of raw materials and the client base, but it is not essential, and indeed unwise, to go into unnecessary detail.

Techniques used in case studies and the value of triangulation

A characteristic feature of case studies is that they employ a variety of different techniques. These include questionnaires, interviews, observation and diaries. All the advice about their planning, piloting and execution needs to be followed. Using a number of methods allows you to **triangulate** the research (page 82) and this helps to make it more robust and valid. You can also use the various techniques of triangulation at different stages in the research. You may start with a questionnaire, which identifies certain interesting features that can be examined in more detail at later interviews. Questionnaires, for example, may ask people about their daily working practices and these can be explored by using a series of focused interviews, and then a set of observation techniques, forming a second and third set of triangulated data collection.

Advantages of a case study approach

The case study is an excellent vehicle for a dissertation. It is an approach that is especially suited to small-scale research and may well appeal to a student carrying out an in-house dissertation. Some advantages are the following:

- It can be carried out by the single researcher.
- It is relatively cheap and not dependent on expensive technology.
- A case study will always generate empirical data and information; you will not be solely dependent on published work. The data may not be present in vast amounts, but it will be interesting and specific to the example under scrutiny.
- It takes place in a natural setting within an actual organization. This gives the work a 'reality' that is often absent from surveys and similar types of investigation. A case study looks at the whole situation and the researcher (you) see the inter-relations as they happen. This background is useful when you come to write up the work.

Disadvantages of a case study approach

With a case study approach there are a number of limitations as follows:

- With a single atypical case study it is often difficult to separate out what is unique to the organization involved and what is common to similar organizations.
- The whole issue of generalization needs to be handled with caution. The degree to which you can relate to the general position is often limited. At the writing up stage this caution needs to be stated quite clearly. It is essential that the generalizations arise from the research carried out, rather than what you think might be the case. Case study research tends to be subjective, but it is a good idea to keep the word 'objective' or at the least 'impartial' in mind when writing up.
- Case studies can generate a lot of information, since each different method used produces its own findings. The analysis and interpretation need to be handled carefully and in a very logical, systematic way. Again, when done effectively, this strengthens the academic argument you are presenting.

As previously stated, case studies are a powerful tool, as well as a methodology, in a wide range of business management situations. So much so that 'case study' has generated an industry in its own right, as a medium for consultancy, and as an advisory service in project management. A good example at this time of writing is an online portfolio describing the international work of a Canadian firm engaged in corporate business management and consultancy. It offers, as described by Friedmann (2011), an example of global reach utilizing technology in an increasingly 'flat world'. A series of case studies are presented describing how this firm organizes its work across three key areas for project management to support organizations. It helps in reducing the risk and uncertainty in launching, accelerating and maintaining change transformation in a range of functional areas (see http://www .schroeder-inc.com/casestudy.html). A similar example involving the UK Government Cabinet Office of the Civil Service can be found at http://www.best-management-practice.com. Here case study is used as a basis for disseminating best management practice products as *'flexible, practical and effective guidance, drawn from a range of the most successful global business experiences'*.

Action research

In recent years action research has attracted a lot of interest. Most of what is written about it concerns educational contexts, focusing particularly upon teachers and the teaching–learning process. Less has been written about action research and management, although Gill and Johnson (2010) give a useful account. Action research is a methodology that can be easily misunderstood. Consider for instance the following three definitions:

> The study of a social setting involving the participants themselves as researchers with a view to improve the quality of action within it. (Rapoport, 1970)

> Action research is small-scale intervention in the functioning of the real world and a close examination of the effects of such intervention. (Halsey, 1972)

> The study of a social situation with a view to improving the quality of action within it. (Elliott, 1980)

What is implicit in all three is that the researcher is interventionist in the research. The research is linked to a plan of action to bring about a change, which in turn brings about an improvement. In other words, action research is about a professional (e.g. manager) studying their own practice in order to improve it. For this to work, there needs to be constant reflection of the issues being considered and the results from this reflection should then feed back into the research. The whole process is cyclic, and this, together with the critical reflection, is needed to identify and implement any improvements and changes, all of which make it a very time-consuming process. Action research, conducted properly, requires a research design that includes a substantial time frame, a clearly identified group of participants located in a specific work-related setting, and an organizational framework, i.e. a group involved in a shared, clearly stated enterprise.

Action research is like case study work in that one situation is studied by using a number of different data collection methods. It is, however, different in that the concept of improvement is always present and mandatory. Action research because of its nuanced complexity is probably mostly associated with doctoral research. There are, however, certain situations, where action research could be an excellent research strategy for a Masters dissertation. For example, part-time students working in companies or an educational setting. A common theme present in action research is the management of change over time and how it involves people. This means issues of confidentiality, access and the difficulty of remaining detached, are present and need to be taken on board during the research. A good source for an overview of more recent developments with this methodology in what is now sometimes called 'participatory action research' is Ozanne and Saatcioglu (2008).

A suggested method for carrying out action research

The whole process is cyclic and uses techniques such as interviews, focus groups, diaries and observation. It is concerned with planned and evaluated interventions that involve groups or individuals who want to improve their professional practice. A number of different models on how to conduct the research have been described along the following lines. The research normally takes place in 4 to 5 stages depending on the problem being investigated.

STAGE 1 – THE START

Here the issues involved are identified, and the problem for improvement is looked at from a variety of standpoints. This stage is about gathering information. The literature is searched and as much information as possible about the situation in question is collected and sifted through to set the research within context.

STAGE 2 – PLAN OF ACTION

Using a number of appropriate data collection methods, more detail is gathered and evaluated. As a result, a plan of action to improve the problem is worked out.

STAGE 3 – ACT, OBSERVE AND MONITOR

The action plan is put into practice and all changes noted. Again a number of methods are used (e.g. interviews, observation) to collect evidence about the success or otherwise of the introduced plan.

STAGE 4 – REFLECT

The effects of the action plans are subjected to critical reflection. This forms the basis for further planning, action and review. The critical reflection needs to be carried out in a systematic way and one method is to ask a series of questions. The type of question will vary depending on the research, but could be along the following lines:

- What are the salient features of this issue or problem?
- Why is it an issue or problem in the first place?
- What outcome(s) would you regard as desirable?
- What actions do you think will deliver these outcomes?
- Why do you think these actions will achieve these outcomes?

STAGE 5 – REPEAT STAGES 2–4

Using the evidence and results from the reflection, the action plan is changed and the whole process starts again in order to bring about continued improvement.

Finally, as with all academic research, the work is written up. As this type of research is a very fluid and continuous process involving repeated cyclic action and critical reflections, it is difficult and often felt inappropriate to write it up in the conventional dissertation layout. It is perhaps better to produce a historical account – a story or narrative format that describes and recounts how the research developed over time. Provided all the salient features of academic writing are present, the literature cited and other academic criteria satisfied, then all should be fine. It would be essential at different points during the research to repeatedly discuss this with your supervisor.

In summary, action research provides an opportunity to do something that is very relevant as a form of applied research. Note, however, it should always result in some action and some research even though the balance between the two can vary in different studies. Sometimes the research element is based on conveying the understandings of the whole picture to all the people involved in a situation. In this context the research outcomes would include an account of the processes carried out, the rationale for actions taken, the perceptions of those involved, the data on which the conclusions are drawn and, if appropriate, the relationship to the work of similar studies.

Like all approaches to research, action research has its limitations. It is not appropriate for making any easy generalizations that might apply to the wider population as a whole, and there is a danger that the researcher becomes too involved in the whole process. Its strength, however, lies in the understanding it can provide to a particular case, and in helping to facilitate an improvement in that situation.

Qualitative research method: Tools and techniques

This section looks at how to go about gathering qualitative data and the importance of always ensuring an alignment between method, purpose and data collection. Three principal methods for qualitative data collection are the interview, observation and diary. The use of observation is also linked by way of example to **ethnography**, a methodology increasingly used to explore the world of a business organization.

The interview

An interview is perhaps the most popular form of qualitative data collection and can provide, when properly conducted, a rich source of material. Take account in the first instance of the pros and cons with using interview as a research tool.

Advantages of interviews

Interviews can be used in a variety of contexts and situations and in conjunction with other research methods. For example, a preliminary interview may identify problems that can either be incorporated into a questionnaire or form the basis of a later and more searching interview. The type of interview will depend on the nature of information you want to collect, and it may range from a highly structured pre-designed list of questions to a free-ranging conversation. The real benefit of an interview is that you are face-to-face with the interviewee, so you can clear up any misunderstandings immediately. Either side can question what they do not understand. Also, during the interview the researcher can re-word or re-order the questions if something unexpected happens and so further explore the unexpected. This needs to be handled with care, as distraction in the form of a 'red herring' can mean proliferation of irrelevant or pointless information.

Disadvantages of interviews

They are very time-consuming. You need to take into account length of interview, travelling to and from interview, transcription of recordings, notes, etc. As a result, you may only interview a small sample that may not be representative of the population. You need to be sure the interview is the best way to get the infor-mation you want.

Moreover, with all interviews there are problems of **bias**, **reliability** and **validity** that must be addressed throughout the whole interview process. Be aware, for instance, of the interviewee who wants to please the interviewer and, as a result, may not say it as they see it. The interviewer must ensure that their personal views and, as a result, bias do not creep in when the interview informa-tion is being evaluated and interpreted. The interviewer–interviewee relationship is very important and it is essential that the whole process be carefully planned. Finally, remember a friendly spontaneous chat with either a friend or group of people does not constitute an interview. The latter is a systematic set of ques-tions tied to a specific purpose or research intention.

Interview preparation

The following checklist highlights the main points to think about when planning interviews.

1. Know the background well and decide if the interview technique is the best way to get the information you need. For example, details about the organization, management structure of a company, or its financial situation may be obtained from annual reports and other company literature, often already in the public domain. An interview can be used to investigate the views of the employees on how the structure works in practice and whether senior management takes on board their opinions about it. Thorough planning at the start is essential.

2. Decide on the type of interview you want: individual, group, telephone, structured or unstructured (sometimes termed in-depth interviews). Quanti-tative research as part of a survey design might also use an interview as a tool in data collection, but the respondent's answers are coded numerically and then analyzed mathematically.

3. Decide how you intend to select potential interviewees. Once chosen, it is a good idea to brief them thoroughly about the format the interview will take. Make arrangements to let them read the final dissertation if they want to as a benefit of participating in the research. You need to develop a rapport with the people taking part. Always be honest and well mannered and use your common sense – this will take you a long way. Remember the people being interviewed are giving up their time and doing you a favour. Also there may be a good age gap between you as a student and the interviewee, so never patronize or show condescension.

4. Decide exactly what you want to ask. Devise the structure and order the questions for structured interviews. With more free-ranging unstructured interviews a prompt list of the topics you want to discuss is needed. Most interviews take the form of what is called a semi-structured interview. The interviewer uses a questions schedule to structure the interview. The schedule may often take the form of several key questions reflecting a set of pre-identified themes, with sub-questions serving as prompts to further facilitate the interviewee's response. It is a good idea to ask more than one question about the same topic; this helps cross-check and correlate validity of answers. It is also a good idea to mix the form of questions. At the beginning use **closed questions** (i.e. ones which can be answered with a 'Yes' or a 'No') and lead up to more **open questions** at the end (e.g. 'What are your views on …'). Open questions can usually probe more sensitive areas. Remember, do not use specialized terminology or jargon, and use everyday language the interviewee can understand. Consider the age of the interviewee. An eighty-year-old discussing working conditions may use a very different vocabulary from someone in their mid-twenties.

5. Be clear about the type of information you want. For example, is it personal background (e.g. age, marital status, education, work experience) or behavioural detail (e.g. what they did in the past, what they are doing now and what they would like to do in the future?), or opinion you need (e.g. how do they feel about a subject?). It helps to divide the questions up into topic areas. This makes later interpretation much easier.

6. Always pilot the final list of questions and topics on a small sample of people. This ensures the questions are clear to understand and helps remove ambiguity. A pilot session will also help you time the interview.

7. Consider how you intend to analyze the information you collect. This may influence how the questions are asked in the first place and should make the whole procedure a lot more straightforward. A look at Chapter 8 may help.

8. Choose a non-threatening environment for the interview, free from distractions and interruptions. This is not easy if you are visiting the interviewee at work.

9. Make sure all official channels are sorted out. A letter from your supervisor explaining about your course and the part played by the dissertation often resolves any issue around access.

10. Don't make the interview too long – tell the interviewee the estimated time and stick to it.

11. How will you record the information: will you use a voice recorder, camcorder, notes or checklist? You will need to obtain consent, and be aware that some people find whatever form of recording used intimidating. Remember, although recording ensures accuracy, transcribing material is time-consuming and can be expensive.

12. Finally, keep an accurate and full record of all the stages involved. This includes how you decided on the type of interview, the selection of the interviewees, choosing the questions to ask, and recording the responses – in fact you should make detailed notes on the whole process from start to finish. This can all be written up and forms an important part of the methodology section in the final dissertation.

Types of interview

Interviews either take place with individuals or groups of people.

1. Personal interviews

Interviews with individuals are known as personal interviews, and can either be structured or unstructured. Each will be described in turn. In a structured personal interview the interviewer has a list of prescribed questions for the interviewee. The advantage of this technique is that you can conduct a larger number of interviews, since the data collected is easier to interpret.

In unstructured personal interviews the interview takes the form of a discussion, and the interviewer directs the conversation by identifying a number of topics and allows the interviewee to talk them through in their own time. This type of interview provides a great deal of information, but the main disadvantage is often in interpreting the material collected. It can also take up more time than a structured interview so usually a smaller number of interviews are carried out. Unstructured interviews are excellent where the aim is to understand the perspective of the interviewee and the personal meanings they attach to different situations.

2. Group interviews

In certain instances you may wish to interview a group of people about a particular topic, for example, their opinions about senior management and how decisions are made in a company. You tend to act as a prompt and direct the general discussion. Group interviews are sometimes termed *focus groups* and the interviewer is called the *moderator*. With this type of interview it is important to have a list of topics that you intend to discuss or the whole session may lose direction and become disorganized. With group interviews you need to be aware of group dynamics and ensure that one person does not take over the discussion at the expense of other members in the group. In this situation you must encourage all members of the group to respond. Questions like 'Do you agree with Matthew's opinion, Margaret?' may help Margaret to join in. However, with group interviews you must never embarrass any member of the group or make them feel inferior or ill at ease.

There are many well known variations of the group interview technique. These include *cognitive mapping* which is a specialized group interview that takes place in an action research setting. It is used a lot in strategic planning, for example, when a group of managers is faced with an issue to resolve. The *critical incident technique* is also used in interview sessions. In this activity, the people being interviewed talk about a specific incident, which they regard as critical and which may have brought about significant changes in their lives.

Carrying out the interview

When carrying out interviews the following checklist should help.

- It is important at the start to establish the nature of the relationship. Thank the interviewee(s) for agreeing to be interviewed. Explain the background and format of the interview and whether you are going to ask a series of specific questions (i.e. you are going to carry out a structured interview) or have a discussion about a series of related topics (i.e. an unstructured interview).
- It is essential at the start to confirm confidentiality, especially if there are sensitive issues involved.
- Non-verbal contact, such as nodding, facial expression, eye contact, smiling and showing interest, is important, and can often make the interviewee more at ease. You need to demonstrate empathy and even how you dress must be appropriate to the occasion.
- Confirm how long the interview will take and stick to it. If recording, ask for permission.
- At the end of the interview it is a good idea to run quickly through the answers. This helps you to sum up the main points and check on the

accuracy of the answers. It may trigger other issues the interviewee(s) may want to mention. Always allow some time at the end for any other comments the interviewee(s) would like to make.

- Finally, listen to what is said. It is the interviewee's ideas and opinions you want – you know yours!

At the end, while everything is still fresh in your memory, go over the interview to make sure you understand any notes. Write down any other comments and impressions you have; it will help at the interpretation stage.

Observation and ethnography

Ethnography is a distinctive qualitative methodology. It is closely associated with research in sociology and social psychology, and widely used in social sciences research. Ethnography is increasingly regarded as a major qualitative mode of inquiry into social and cultural conditions, not only in the academic social sciences, but increasingly in organizations and activities outside a university. Ethnography, as a method utilizing participant-observation, interviewing, and other qualitative techniques, is regarded as a good fit for the study of unpredictable outcomes, complex emerging social formations, and technological and market change. It is mentioned here because it is a third, but more widely applied methodology, in what is an even more widely ranging take-up of sociological research.

It could be argued that the most obvious method of data collection in any real life setting is observation; an accurate record of what people do and say in real-life situations. In fact, one of the most influential management gurus, Henry Mintzberg, made his reputation by writing about his observations on what senior managers did during their normal working day. Mintzberg spent a week in five middle- to large-sized organizations (a consulting firm, a technology company, a hospital, a school, and a consumer goods company) observing how the senior executive in each occupied their time. Mintzberg's book (*The Nature of Managerial Work*), published in 1973, is a seminal text and well worth a read on how the technique of observation can be used to best effect.

Observation is a good method to use in the area of business. It lends itself to many different situations and is popular with students carrying out dissertations in their workplace. Correctly applied, it can be very effective with dissertation research.

The success of observation as a technique depends on a number of factors. These include the accurate reporting and description of the topic under investigation, free access to all aspects of the investigation and plenty of time for the observations to take place.

When carrying out observation you must have a thorough background of the situation being researched. It is essential to identify exactly the sort of information you want to observe, everything from general features to specific detail. You have to record a lot of material, and this may range from what people say to one another to how they behave and what they actually do in their job. In addition, non-verbal information, for instance how they look and dress, may have a bearing on the subject being researched. Observation takes place in real-life situations, so you need to be alert to sudden changes that may influence or inform the research.

Types of observation

There are two broad ways in which observation in a research project can be carried out. There is *participant observation* and *non-participant observation* (sometimes termed *structured observation*). Either can be carried out with everyone knowing about the research (i.e. *overt observation*) or in secret, with no-one in the know (i.e. *covert observation*). Some investigators claim that when people know they are being observed they behave and act differently and, as a result, covert observation is preferable. Also, in certain types of social science research, for example on the behaviour of inmates in prison, or as a member of a small deviant group, covert research may be the only way to gather meaningful data. Covert studies obviously raise a number of ethical issues.

Participant observation

Participant observation refers to a technique where the researcher becomes completely involved in the situation that is being researched. An example might be a theme park where on certain days a particular roller coaster ride is less popular, in spite of the fact that the same numbers of people are admitted to the park. The difference in popularity seems to correspond to days when there is a changeover of staff in charge of the ride. The researcher could join the workforce on the roller coaster and, hopefully, at first hand, be able to investigate the reasons for the change in popularity. This type of research emphasizes gathering 'intelligence' and an interpretation of events and the interaction of the people involved. Research of this type employs observation that focuses upon the behaviour of people in a specific cultural context. It is a very popular technique of ethnographic researchers.

There are, however, a number of general points to bear in mind if you are thinking about this type of data collection. First, you need to gain access and enter the research setting. If the research is covert then you become like an actor playing a part; you must not reveal your true identity. If you arouse suspicion as to your true identity, this could generate a hostile reaction and affect the overall validity of your work.

If the research is open and the people around you know you are carrying out the work, then your interpersonal skills need to be excellent in order for you to gain their trust. Secondly, you need to monitor your conduct during the research; be polite, respectful and interested in what is happening; you need to empathize.

How you record the data during participant observation can be difficult and this needs to be thought about before the research starts. Do you take notes, use a voice recorder, or use checklists? With the roller coaster research as an example you would look for any activity that may affect people going on the ride. This could be a member of staff being rude to potential customers or some disagreement between staff that may result in there being fewer people on the ride, but you need to consider just how you record it. Finally, when the data collection is over, you need to leave the research setting. This withdrawal can be just as difficult as gaining access in the first place – particularly if you are sitting at the top of a roller coaster!

Non-participant (structured) observation

This is where the observer remains clearly detached from the situation. You do not join in, but record what is happening. With the roller coaster example you may record the time it takes people to get on and off the ride. Perhaps one of the attendants on the low popularity days manages this procedure in a slightly different way. Over the day the reason for the lower number of people on the ride becomes clear. The drop in the number of customers is not connected with the ride's popularity, but with the way it is managed by the two workforce groups on different days.

When carrying out this type of observation it is essential that you 'blend into the background' and don't let your presence get in the way. Try to position yourself in an out-of-the-way place and don't engage in long conversations with the people you are observing. Experience has shown that the longer you are in a setting the more your presence is accepted and the less obvious you become.

Ways of recording the observations

There are two popular ways for recording observations: these are the diary method and the use of checklists, as explained below.

1. The diary

The keeping of a diary or log is an excellent way to record participant observation. Robson (1993) recommends that it may be written up in two sections. The first part, known as the *descriptive observation,* systematically reports on the events that take place, the characters involved, conversations that occur, together with a description of the setting, e.g. office, meeting room, etc. Don't forget to include the obvious, such as time and date. These accounts should be completed as soon as possible while events are fresh in the memory. With overt research you may be able to make quick notes as you go along (field notes) and/ or use a small recorder to dictate notes as long as this is done discreetly – notes of this sort can prove very useful later in the process of data management. With a covert study you will probably have to rely on your memory.

A second stage in keeping an observation diary is what Robson termed the *narrative account.* Here you reflect on the events and begin to identify ideas and trends arising from the descriptions. This early analysis and interpretation may alert you to particular issues which need to be observed again or which you have overlooked and which need to be included in following observations. The diary keeping should be a reflective process and it is sometimes termed *analytical induction.*

It is often difficult to stand back at this stage in forming a series of interpretive comments and remain impartial or be objective. One technique that in our own experience helps, is to imagine you are reading the diary of someone else, and study it as if you were carrying out research on that person. For example, suppose you were researching the ideas of a well-known management guru: reading their personal diary would give you an insight into how they developed their management ideas. It can also help if you write the description in the first person, but the narrative in the third person. It takes practice to keep a good diary, so some early attempts such as recording and reflecting one week in your life are good ways to begin. A diary can be a data collection method in its own right. This is explained on pages 58–59.

2. Using checklists

With non-participant or structured observation you can use checklists, sometimes referred to as an *observation schedule.* Include in the schedule the type of features you want to record. These may include particular events, their frequency and duration. For instance, if you were observing a meeting you would have a seating plan, or when individuals spoke you would note the content and manner of their contribution. Was it friendly, challenging, did they agree or disagree with one another? You would also record the people who said nothing.

It is possible to buy ready-made schedules, but these tend to be expensive and may not suit your particular needs. If you decide to make your own, it is essential you choose the type of incident you need to include. An examination of the literature will help by alerting you to some of the key issues linked to the topic. It is important to be as focused as possible. You don't have the time to record everything, only be alert to what you need. A **pilot study** to iron out any problems and ambiguities is essential. The skills associated with observation, identification of different categories of data and physically recording this data can be tricky. Try to make sure you can practise beforehand.

Advantages of observational research

These include the following:

- It is cheap, you can do it on your own, and it does not need expensive complex technology.
- It usually works since you always observe something. Many people don't like to be interviewed and often throw postal questionnaires away.
- You experience a situation at first hand and this may give you a better insight when you interpret the data.
- Observation is a useful technique to research an organization of which you are a part, for example, when you work in a company.

Disadvantages of observational research

These include the following:

- It is a time-consuming process and this needs to be borne in mind at the planning stage. Remember, dissertations have deadlines that must be met.
- With participant observation the researcher may become so involved in the situation that the research can take second place.
- You may witness and record situations that you do not agree with or hear conversations where you think one party is obviously to blame. Personal bias in these situations needs to be guarded against and managed.

Indirect observation

In addition to formal observation techniques described, other information may be observed as a result of just being in an organization. This could include, for example, notices, minutes of meetings, letters and correspondence. You may also hear internal gossip about various parts of the organization. All this type of information from *indirect observation* provides a context in which you can set your research. Properly used, it can inform the research and certainly help when you come to interpret your results.

A research diary: more ethnographic method?

Keeping a research diary is not only a useful way of recording observation. It is often used as a method in its own right as well as a useful data collection technique. You can either write a diary yourself, or ask people involved in an investigation to keep one so they can note down their ideas and reflect on personal circumstance and attitudes. Diaries are excellent when investigating the culture of an organization and changes within it, for example, at times of mergers and big re-structuring exercises. They are good to elicit opinion about different styles of management and leadership in an organization.

Diaries kept by other people ensure you collect information directly from respondents and several different writers' work can be compared on completion of the research. Also, the researcher has time to do other things. There are, however, disadvantages with asking people to keep diaries. They need to write reasonably well, and often require help at the start as to the sort of things they should record and how often they have to make an entry in their diary. They need constant encouragement that they are collecting information about the right things. Obviously anything they write is in confidence and this should be respected throughout the investigation. When asking other people to keep a diary, the following guidance may help:

- At the start give a short informal presentation about yourself and the aims of the research.
- Provide a checklist of what you need in each diary entry: date, time, location, a description of events.
- Encourage volunteers to write the diary every day, while events are fresh in the memory. It is the content that is important – you are not in the business of correcting spelling and grammar.
- Encourage reflection about the issues being researched as well as a factual recall of a day's work. Some practice sessions here as a group will be beneficial and help build confidence. The techniques described for the observation diary (pages 58–59) may assist. As with all aspects of data collection, this early preparation needs to be written up and included in the final dissertation. It corresponds to the pilot stage used in questionnaire design.

Finally, a separate personal research diary or journal can be a useful tool for the researcher. In fact, many UK universities have adopted a policy of requiring doctoral students to keep a research journal. The keeping of a research diary would actually help all dissertation students. The diary can be used to record and comment upon stages in the research project including key planning, supervision and significant events. It is also used to record a process of 'reflexive reflection'. A good example of this approach is explained as a tool for learning, and builds upon pedagogic research carried out at the University of Lancaster. Details can be found at the University College London's website http://www.ucl.ac.uk/teaching-learning/training-development/phd-supervisor-development/phd_diaries.

Dissertation tips

Finally, here are some tips to think about when working through the kinds of qualitative methods or approaches to use in your research design.

- Keep it simple. When selecting tools for your research approach go for a straightforward fit between your topic, methodology and method. Don't make it over-complicated.
- Look for the unexpected or unlikely result in the data collected and be ready to score high for originality in your research but then test your findings by applying the 'refutability principle'. In other words, make sure your results can't be challenged or disproved.
- Look for the anticipated or expected and score high for plausibility and credibility in your interpretation of the research findings, but then test your conclusions by applying the 'constant comparative' principle. Does your work agree with that of other researchers in the same field?
- Make meaningful use of the new technologies when they enhance data quality or help to manage process: for example, you might use digital or visual recording of data in an interview or observation; and again, computerized software for the data analysis and construction of the report – not just because you can buy it or use it.
- Start and keep writing. Try and write up as you go along. Have a quick look at Chapter 9 about writing up your dissertation. Draft an early contents page and use it as a 'road map'. Begin, or maintain a research journal and draft out the various stages of the dissertation including drafts of the *Introduction, Literature review, Methodology*, etc. Sketch out the *Results* chapter and produce a working plan for the management of data within the project. Share any or all of these with your supervisor.

Summary

This chapter has focused on the various aspects of qualitative research, and reviewed its strengths when applied to business and management research.

The key points included in this chapter are:

- The nature of the qualitative paradigm.
- The role of case study research: its features, advantages and disadvantages.
- The nature and use of action research.
- The tools and techniques of qualitative research, including interviews and observational research.
- The use of a research diary as a data collection method in its own right.
- Some helpful tips when carrying out qualitative research.

5 The quantitative paradigm: techniques, including sampling and triangulation

Introduction

An overview of quantitative research was given in Chapter 3. Quantitative methods have their historical origins in science and the approach is sometimes referred to as the '**scientific method**'. It is based on the collection of facts and observable phenomena, and scientists use these to deduce scientific laws and establish relationships. Research in business and management also uses quantitative methods and these can provide a more objective base to certain aspects of professional practice.

Quantitative research describes, explains and tests relationships. In particular, it examines cause-and-effect relationships. The diagnostic feature is that the techniques used always generate numerical data which is then analysed. The analysis can be simple in mathematical terms involving the production of tables, charts and diagrams (e.g. **pie chart, bar chart**, etc.). This type of interpretation is referred to as **descriptive statistics**. Depending on your dissertation this level of analysis is often sufficient. Data analysis can be more complicated and involve mathematical procedures and statistical tests of significance. This is termed **inferential statistics**. Although software packages (e.g. IBM SPSS Statistics, Minitab) are now available which carry out all the calculations, you still need to understand the underlying principles of any methods you use.

As previously noted, you are not expected to use every technique available, only the ones most suitable to your dissertation. With quantitative research, especially if mathematical and statistical procedures are involved, you must feel confident in using them. If you need inferential statistics, and mathematics is not one of your strengths, you would be well advised to get extra help before you start. It is essential with any method that you fully understand all the implications. As highlighted earlier, a 'mix' of qualitative and quantitative techniques to research a topic is a good thing. It provides a range of perspectives to interpret a topic. Qualitative methods are sometimes used to help understand and supplement the results and conclusions generated by quantitative techniques. The combination of a qualitative and quantitative approach is referred to as 'mixed method' research. This is discussed on page 37.

A type of dissertation which could use quantitative techniques is one on marketing, where the effectiveness of different marketing strategies is compared. Another example could be a dissertation researching the introduction of a new senior management structure into an organization; the effects before and after the introduction could be investigated. A quantitative approach is often used in studies where the financial positions of different companies are compared and financial trends, stock market values and implications are examined.

In business and management dissertations, the two main methods used to collect numerical data are **surveys** and **experiments**. Before they are described, the general features of quantitative techniques are explained.

General points about quantitative data collection techniques

Quantitative research sets up a **hypothesis** or theory. This is a proposition which is tested and, depending on the results of the test, the hypothesis or theory is either accepted or rejected. This type of research is deductive in that from the general situation, inferences can be made about a specific example. In other words, you start with a theory which applies in every case and the data collected either supports or rejects the theory. Quantitative research is, therefore, often termed **hypothetico-deductive**.

The emphasis is on counting, measurement and testing. Numbers and numerical analysis are always involved. Numbers alone (e.g. 5, 15, 34, etc.), however, mean very little. They need to be defined by a particular unit. For example, units can be length (e.g. metres), or position (e.g. 3rd, 4th, etc.), or time (e.g. hours, seconds). It is essential at the planning and pilot stage to decide the form the results will take and how you intend to analyze them. Be clear in your own mind what has to be either counted or measured. If any type of statistical analysis (e.g. chi-square) is used, then you must decide at the start which tests to use; most tests will only work with certain types of data. The number of samples needed and the size of each sample also influences the choice of test. All this needs to be incorporated into the overall research design. This will strengthen the design and in turn support the **validity** of any conclusions. Too many researchers only think about results and what to do with them when the research is up and running. Time spent at the planning stage is never wasted – it will be included in the final write-up.

If possible, as you go along, quickly draw tables and make calculations, etc. This will give some idea as to the general trend the results are taking, and may alert you to the need for extra results. As mentioned above many computer programs are now available which will draw out various figures and make calculations. If you are allowed to use them and they are available, they save a great deal of time.

Types of data

Quantitative data is either *discrete* (e.g. the number of cars a factory produces in one day is a definite number, i.e. 1, 2 or 3, etc.; it cannot be 3.5), or *continuous* (the amount of flour milled in a factory can be of any weight). **Discrete data** is always counted and **continuous data** is measured.

It is important to decide which scale of measurement you are going to use before you collect any data as certain statistical tests can be used with certain types of data. The scales of data are as follows:

- Data may be *nominal* or *categorical,* e.g. cars in a car park can be sorted according to make, and respondents in a survey may be male or female. The data is put into a category – it is essential that the categories are quite distinct and data cannot be put into more than one. In a questionnaire **nominal** or **categorical data** could be collected by the following type of question:

> Are you male or female? Please ring the appropriate word.

- Data may be *ordinal,* which means the data is on a scale with both classification and rank. The data is sorted and then put into some sort of order. For example, a political party selects candidates and then conducts a popularity poll. The results of the poll are Mr Matthews 34 per cent, Mr Holmes 45 per cent and Mr Thompson 21 per cent. When set in order Mr Holmes is first, Mr Matthews second and Mr Thompson third. The 1–3 scale is the ordinal scale. An ordinal scale implies order, so in a questionnaire an ordinal question might read:

> How well do you rate your line manager? Please circle the most appropriate number.
>
> | Very good | Good | Fair | Poor | Very poor |
> |-----------|------|------|------|-----------|
> | 1 | 2 | 3 | 4 | 5 |

Note: Nominal (categorical) and ordinal data can only be used with non-parametric statistical tests (page 151).

- *Interval* **data** is where a scale is used and there are equal differences between points on the scale, but there is no true zero. It is arbitrary. An example of interval data is time. Modern time is measured from 1AD, but time did not start here. In a questionnaire an interval data question might read:

> How many years have you worked for this company? Please enter the number of years in the space provided. ...

- *Ratio* **data** is similar to interval data in that there are equal differences between points on the scale, but there is a true zero. Runners in a race all start from the same starting line which is regarded as zero.

  Length is an example of ratio data. In a questionnaire a ratio scale question could read:

> How many metres of fabric has your factory produced today? Please enter the number of metres in the space provided. ...

Note: Interval and ratio data can only be used with parametric statistical tests (page 153).

It is very likely with quantitative research that some of your results will be stored in a computerized database. If you intend to keep information about the people involved in your research on a database and it is possible, from the information stored, to identify them then you must comply with the Data Protection Acts. Most large organizations, like universities, have a Data Protection Officer who should be able to offer advice and information about data protection. In the UK it is the Ministry of Justice that is responsible for data protection issues. Their website address is http://www.justice.co.uk

Techniques of data collection

Surveys

A survey is a popular way of researching and explaining some aspect of a population. Surveys are used, for example, in market research, opinion surveys, customer feedback and attitude surveys. Surveys are carried out by either interviews or questionnaires, or both. It is usually impossible, because of time, cost, size, etc., to consult every member of the population (termed the **sampling frame**), and a sample is, therefore, chosen. In most cases, a sample must be typical of the population and unbiased. Statisticians have developed techniques like random sampling, systematic sampling and stratified sampling to reduce bias and help ensure reliability. Sampling is explained in more detail on page 76.

It is now possible to use online packages to plan and arrange a survey for you. They will even find an appropriate sample of respondents, carry out the survey and send you the final results. Two well-known examples are SurveyMonkey (http://www.surveymonkey.com) and Bristol Online Surveys (http://www.survey .bris.ac.uk). This type of service is used by many multinational companies. It can be expensive, although your university may have an account with an online survey provider. Since nearly all the work is done for you it's worth checking with your supervisor if you can use this type of package. Even if you can use them then knowledge of the stages in constructing a survey is still essential so you fully understand what's involved.

Interviews

Although interviews are mainly used when taking a qualitative approach (page 41) it is possible to code numerically the findings from interviews, so they can be used in quantitative research.

Questionnaires

For our purposes a questionnaire is regarded as a series of questions, each one providing a number of alternative answers from which the respondents can choose. Questionnaires are widely used in business, and popular with dissertation students. Although it seems obvious that if you want to know something from someone, you ask them a question, in reality the procedures involved in designing, writing and administrating questionnaires are complex. As with all aspects of research, never underestimate the amount of planning required. Again, thorough background knowledge via searching the literature is essential.

Questionnaires generate data in a very systematic and ordered fashion. The responses to the questions are quantified, categorized and subjected to statistical analysis. At the planning stage decide which kind of analysis (either descriptive or inferential statistics) you intend to use; this will determine the way the questionnaire is designed.

Irrespective of the format, there are general points about questionnaires and their construction which apply to all. They are as follows:

- The quality of a questionnaire ultimately depends on the quality of the questions. Good and easy to understand questions will engage the respondents and encourage accurate replies.

- Be clear in your own mind why you are using a questionnaire in the first place. Decide exactly what your research objectives are. What type of information do you want to collect from the questionnaire? List all the areas about which information is needed. It may be easier to collect the data from an already published source.

- Choose whether to use postal or self-administered questionnaires.

- Keep questions as simple as possible; each question should only deal with one issue.

- A good attractive layout will encourage a reply. The questionnaire should be as short as possible and not excessive in length. This means you must think carefully about what you want each question to ask.

- Ask straightforward and unambiguous questions first. Start with questions about age, education and occupation and then lead up to more sensitive issues.

- Use **'closed' questions** like 'Do you smoke?' where the response is straightforward. The answer is either 'Yes' or 'No'. Closed questions are quick to answer and easy to code for later analysis.

- Use 'open' questions where you need opinions. For example, 'Have you any comments to make about the finance department of the organization?' With this type of question, although subsequent coding is more complex, you can be alerted to important issues which could be followed up in a second questionnaire or interview. If you want to gauge a degree of opinion, then ranking questions using a Likert or rating scale may be used. An example is the line manager question already given to illustrate the ordinal scale.

- Group questions into sub-headings; each sub-heading can contain questions about similar topics.

- Avoid vague questions like 'Are you satisfied with your job?' The word 'satisfy' can have a number of meanings. Don't use specialized vocabulary, unless you are sure it will be understood by the respondents. The wording of questions is very important; you should never lead or patronize.

- Give an example of how a question should be answered with simple instructions on how to complete the questionnaire, e.g. inform respondents to tick boxes, or circle appropriate numbers, etc. Don't be afraid to guide the respondent on how to answer the questions.

- Unless anonymity and confidentiality are required, request the respondent's name, address, email, etc. should you need to contact them, and ask if they would like to be involved later, for example in follow-up interviews.

- With all questionnaires it is essential to include either a covering letter or supporting **rationale**. This should state quite clearly why the questionnaire is being conducted, and who is doing it. You could explain that you are a university student researching a particular topic and the questionnaire is form-ing part of your dissertation. You should give access and allow them to read the final dissertation. Finally, thank them for their help in completing the ques-tionnaire and assure them their privacy will be maintained if this is requested.

- Practise how you intend to analyse any information from the questionnaires in terms of either descriptive or inferential statistics. As stated above it is important that the method of data analysis is decided right at the start. From experience, if this is not sorted out, it will cause a lot of trouble at a later stage, and can even invalidate any results.
- With all questionnaires it is essential that a pilot is carried out with a small number of volunteers. A pilot questionnaire will identify the ambiguous questions, alert you to problems of analysis and generally make the final version more relevant. As with other aspects of data collection, time spent running the pilot and amending the questionnaire is not wasted. It is all written up and forms part of the **methodology** section of the final dissertation. When running the pilot, if possible, use respondents similar to your intended sample. If this is not possible, then ask a few friends to work through the questionnaires for you. This is better than nothing!

Types of questionnaire

In the main there are two formats for questionnaires:

- *Postal questionnaires.* Questionnaires sent by mail and either returned by mail or collected individually by the researcher. Questionnaires are now being sent using email. Online survey companies use email.
- *Self-administered and telephone questionnaires.* This is where the questionnaire is filled in by the researcher after asking a respondent a series of questions. This is in a sense a very structured interview and the advice given for interviews still applies. Self-administered questionnaires can some-times be completed using the telephone. Also in certain situations the inter-viewer leaves a questionnaire with a respondent and agrees to call back at a later date and time to collect it.

POSTAL QUESTIONNAIRES

Postal questionnaires are popular with students and they can form the basis of a good dissertation. One of the major problems with a postal questionnaire is the low response rate, and even with a well-planned questionnaire using follow-up request letters and telephone calls, the response rate can remain low. It is, there-fore, essential that when planning a postal questionnaire you decide at the start how to handle and interpret a low rate of return.

One way is to find out as much as you can about the sample of people to whom you are sending the postal questionnaire. Therefore, if responses are only returned from one section of the sample, this may alert you to inferences from parts of the sample who did not respond. For example, some years ago one of the authors (BW) carried out an industrial survey on the manufacturing industries of East Yorkshire and North Lincolnshire, UK and their knowledge of new technologies. In particular, their awareness of genetic engineering and biotechnology, and their potential importance to the manufacturing industry, was investigated. A postal questionnaire involving over 2 000 companies was carried out. Certain manufacturing industries, e.g. engineering, failed to respond, and in the main, replies were received from the pharmaceutical and chemical industries. As a result, follow-up interviews were carried out on the industries which failed to return the initial questionnaire.

Other issues which can be used to help secure a good response rate are:

- The appearance of the questionnaire – it must look attractive; have a spacious layout with plenty of room for questions and answers.
- The wording of the questions must be simple and clear. The contents must be arranged so respondents have an opportunity to express their own views, as well as answering set questions. Every so often, after a block of questions on one topic, a side heading 'Have you any other comments?' will help. Leave space, no more than three lines, for the respondent to add their own comments.
- Instructions on how to complete the questionnaire must be simple, clear and bold. It sometimes helps to have these separately printed on coloured paper.
- Timing is important. If you are sending your questionnaires to senior managers, remember they are busy people. Your questionnaire should take no longer than 5 to 10 minutes at the most to complete.
- Completing the questionnaire should be regarded by the respondent as a learning experience. Early questions should be simple with a high interest value. The questions in the middle can be more difficult and searching. The last few questions should have a high interest value to encourage a return of the completed questionnaire.
- Large market research companies conducting postal questionnaires often offer inducements, such as competitions for cars, etc., hopefully to ensure a response. Unless you are a millionaire student, this scenario would be unlikely. Perhaps a small inducement, such as a teabag attached to the questionnaire with an invitation to take a 5-minute tea break in order to complete the questionnaire, might serve just as well, if not better!

- Use first-class postage and enclose a first-class stamped addressed envelope to encourage a reply.
- If questionnaires are not returned, then a follow-up letter reminding respondents is a good idea. The letter could re-emphasize the importance of the study, and enclose another stamped addressed envelope and a second copy of the questionnaire. Some researchers make this second questionnaire shorter, including only the most essential questions to which they need an answer.

Advantages of postal questionnaires

Some advantages are as follows:

- They are cheap and do not incur expensive travel and accommodation expenses.
- They allow for a large sample spread over a wide area to be surveyed.
- They are a relatively quick way of receiving a response.
- They avoid interview bias. Personal questions are often more willingly answered as the respondent is not face-to-face with the interviewer.

Disadvantages of postal questionnaires

Some disadvantages are as follows:

- As questions tend to be simple, straightforward and not over-complicated, there is not a richness of information that is sometimes collected with other methods.
- You may not receive a spontaneous answer. Respondents may discuss the questions with other colleagues before completing the questionnaire. As all questions are seen before they are answered, the answers cannot always be treated as independent. For example, if the question 'Can you name any dog food on the market?' was asked and the next question was 'Do you feed your dog 'Doggyfood'?', respondents may not have thought of any dog food for the answer to question 1, but could include the brand 'Doggyfood' as the answer after reading question 2.
- You cannot be sure that the named respondent has completed the questionnaire. A busy executive may ask an assistant to complete it on their behalf.

SELF-ADMINISTERED AND TELEPHONE QUESTIONNAIRES

With self-administered and telephone questionnaires you are in direct contact with the respondents and the good practice advocated for interviews (see page 49) applies. If you are going to deliver the form to respondents' homes you need to make arrangements for the collection of the completed forms.

Telephone questionnaires can be useful and you can have the questionnaire already programmed into your computer so you can directly input the responses. This saves time at the data interpretation stage. Computer-assisted telephone interviewing (CATI) can speed up the whole process and can save a lot of time. Automated computer telephone interviewing (ACTI) is similar to CATI, but uses a speaker independent voice recognition system which asks the questions and stores the answers. If these systems are available and you are allowed to use them, then give them a try.

With self-administered questionnaires and CATI it is a good idea to quickly run through the completed questionnaire at the end with the respondent to make sure all questions have been answered.

In summary, carefully planned and administered surveys are an excellent research tool for most dissertations. Figure 5.1 summarizes the main stages involved.

Experiments

An experimental study, often quoted in the literature, is that conducted by Elton Mayo (1933). Mayo investigated how different working conditions, such as lighting, shorter working hours and varied rest breaks (in total ten changes were looked at) affected productivity. The experiments took place in Western Electric's Hawthorne Works in Chicago between 1927 and 1932. The research showed that productivity increased whether the lights were bright or dim, whether the working day was long or short, and so on. The only explanation, Mayo concluded, was that the employees felt part of a team and work group; not simply parts of a machine. During the experiments there had been communication between the workers and the researchers. As a result the workers felt more valued and more responsible both for individual and group performance. This self and group esteem appeared more influential on productivity than any changes in the working environment. Obviously the results surprised the researchers who naturally expected that changes in working conditions would have an effect on productivity. Mayo's work is often quoted, and now an unintended effect as a result of a research experiment, caused by subjects knowing they are part of the experiment, is often referred to as the **Hawthorne effect**.

As can be seen from Mayo's work, experiments are used where the researcher deliberately sets out to control and manipulate all aspects of the situation. There is always a high degree of control. Experiments investigate the relationship between cause and effect. They determine whether a change in one factor (the **independent variable**) causes and produces an effect in another factor (the **dependent variable**). The researcher sets up a situation where the independent

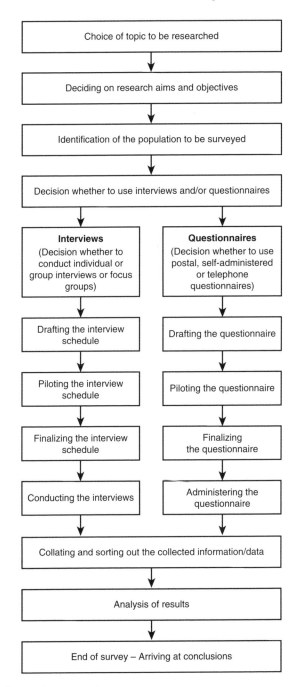

Figure 5.1 Stages in survey design

variable (in some cases there may be more than one) is brought into play and the effect on the dependent variable is recorded as a result. There may be instances where there is more than one independent variable, in which case each one is tested in turn and the effects on the dependent variable noted.

The concept of controls

In science the experimental approach is regarded as the classical method of research. Because of the nature of science, especially in the physical sciences, with laboratories and special equipment, it is possible to have strict controls and even replicate an experiment a number of times. The concept of controls is important in scientific research. If you were, for example, investigating the effect of oxygen in a particular situation, one experiment would be carried out in the presence of oxygen and a second one would take place in the absence of oxygen. The experiment without oxygen is the control, and it provides a comparison as to what happens in the presence of oxygen. You could also repeat the experiments a number of times to determine the validity of the results. In short a control shows that any observed effect is caused by the treatment being studied and not due to some other factors.

Experiments in business and management

Business and management are very different from science in that experiments are not so easy to organize. Large organizations are constantly changing and many of the changes happen only once. Imagine a large company is introducing a new staff appraisal policy. It would be possible to examine the before and after effects, but it would be impossible to repeat the whole introduction.

However, there are times in business research when an experimental approach can be used to good effect. Suppose you are investigating the links between employment and the acquisition of IT skills. Given that IT plays such a major role in business today, you could assume that a person is more likely to be unemployed if their IT skill base is low. An experimental prediction like this is called a hypothesis (not to be confused with the **null** and **alternative hypothesis** used in statistics). An experimental hypothesis is concerned with the relationship between two variables: an independent variable and a dependent variable. With the above example the independent variable is the employment factor and the IT skills level the dependent variable. Two groups of people could be used: one in employment and the other out of work. The IT skill level of each group could be measured and the results collected. On closer inspection the situation is not so clear-cut. There are a number of features, all of which could influence the results. Would it matter if some of the employed were joiners, teachers, or lawyers, or would they need to be in the same job? How would you measure the level of IT skills? Would you expect simple keyboard skills or a deep understanding of programming? Would the age of the people matter and would you need to know the proportion of men to women in the experiment? Finally, how do you know if the results have arisen by chance or because the presence of IT skills can actually affect the chances of employment? Here you may need to use some form of statistical test of significance to strengthen your conclusion that a low IT skill level does affect employability.

Given all the pitfalls, an experimental approach, if carefully applied, can be used with great effect with some dissertations, especially in marketing. Examples of likely titles include 'The sales effectiveness of a new display', 'The impact of a retail price change on market share', and 'The effect of a different package design on sales'. In business and management research the independent variable is often termed as a categorical or classification variable. For instance, in a study to determine the effect of a training programme on staff, the independent variable would be the training programme and the effects it causes the dependent variable.

As with any form of research, if you are going to take an experimental approach, thorough planning, extensive literature searching and careful thought given to the whole process are essential. Experimental design, if correctly used, can produce work of a high quality and is suitable for many business and management dissertations.

Types of experimental design

In practice there are different ways of carrying out an experiment. The one chosen depends on the facilities available and local conditions.

THE ONE-SHOT CASE STUDY

Here the group is exposed to a treatment and this is followed by a measure. An example would be to allow a group of administrators to attend a one-day workshop on report writing skills. After the day if they are more effective at writing, it could be argued that this was the result of the workshop. However, the result could also be due to other things connected with home or other aspects of work, etc. With this type of experiment there is no control or comparison group.

THE ONE-GROUP PRE-TEST POST-TEST DESIGN

Here the subject is pre-tested before the treatment and then tested following the treatment. In other words, if you want to see whether there is a change because of something, it is a good idea to gauge the situation before and after the change happens. In the case of the administrators, some assessment of their writing skills could take place before and after the one-day workshop. Any improvement in their writing skills would strengthen the idea that any differences were caused by their attendance at the workshop. Again, no control or comparison group is used.

THE STATIC GROUP COMPARISON

Using a pre-test can indicate if a change has occurred, but it does not necessarily indicate that the treatment is the reason for the change. In our example the administrators might have seen a programme on TV about effective writing and this could have influenced the results. This can be overcome by having two groups of administrators, and subjecting only one group to the one-day skills writing workshop. In this situation it can be assumed that both groups have had the same outside influences. Therefore if the treatment group responds better it can be assumed that the one-day workshop is having some effect.

The idea of having two groups, one subjected to the treatment (i.e. the workshop) and one not subjected to the treatment, illustrates an important concept with experimental design. It is the use and need for controls. As noted above, in a laboratory controls are easy to arrange, but in real life it is difficult. Some idea of comparison, however, incorporates the concept of a control and this helps strengthen an experimental-type investigation. The argument is strengthened in the example above, if the two groups of administrators are as identical as possible, and chosen at random without bias. The importance of sampling is discussed on page 76.

THE PRE-TEST POST-TEST CONTROL GROUP DESIGN

This form of design is particularly robust. Both groups are pre-tested at the start, one group receives the treatment, the control does not, and both groups are post-tested at the end.

Other types of experimental design

A number of more sophisticated designs are available. Some of them can be quite complex, and more suited to a postgraduate dissertation. One form that may be useful is what is termed the *quasi-experimental approach* (quasi = as if).

It is difficult in the world of business to replicate true experimental conditions. The researcher is not able to manipulate all the variables, controls and other factors which should be present in a true experiment. It may be possible, however, in certain situations to make a good approximation. This is termed a quasi-experimental approach. The concept of control and experimental groups is present, but normally not chosen in a random fashion. Dissertation topics where this form of investigation may be useful, is if you want to research some change that has occurred in an organization. For example, the introduction of flexitime, a new staff appraisal policy, or the changes in staff morale following a re-organization of senior management. With this type of investigation you do get a before and after effect. However, because the procedures are not as precise as with true experimental designs, any results may be subject to wide interpretation.

Procedure for carrying out an experiment

Remember, because of the nature of business and management it is very difficult to give a definitive guide on how to conduct experimental research but the following should get you started. The following scheme has been freely adapted from Creswell (2008).

1. *Identify a problem that is agreeable to the experimental method.* If we look again at some of the examples identified earlier, it could be along the lines of the introduction of a management training programme for personal assistants to senior managers.

2. *Formulate the hypothesis and identify the variables.* With the given example, the hypothesis you want to test could read 'To ascertain whether the introduction of a management training programme will influence the effectiveness of senior management personal assistants'. The independent variable is the management training programme, and the dependent variable will be the effectiveness with respect to the personal assistants. Remember that variables must be measurable, so with this example how would you measure the effectiveness of the training programme? The ways you collect the data at this stage can be various, e.g. interviews, questionnaires, asking the personal assistants to keep diaries, and so on. However, you need to decide how it can be quantified and measured.

3. *Choose the subjects to be tested.* Here we need to choose the personal assistants, and decide whether we choose all of them in an organization, or just a sample. If you decide on a sample you need to think about the sample size and the characteristics of the sample. Would members of the sample be the same age, sex, have similar qualifications, have worked in the company for the same length of time, etc? All these factors could influence the final results. Also, do you intend only to carry out some test on the personal assistants, or are you going to involve senior management in your experiment?

4. *Selection of a suitable experimental design.* You need to select a design which best suits the situation at hand. Let's assume we are dealing with a big company and there are lots of personal assistants and senior managers. In this case the pre-test post-test control group design may be the most appropriate.

5. *Carrying out the experiment, collecting and evaluating the results.* This is perhaps the most challenging and interesting part, and, as with all research, allows the relevant literature to inform your thinking. An experiment can take a lot of time to set up and organize, so may be more suited to postgraduate work. Thorough planning is essential and always carry out a pilot study to identify potential problems.

Sampling

With any form of research such as surveys involving interviews and/or question-naires, it is usually impossible to question every member of the population involved. For example, if your dissertation was about UK DIY retailing you should, in theory, question every DIY outlet in the UK (i.e. you would carry out a **census**). Obviously, this would be impossible to do in the time available, and you would have to confine your research to a limited number of outlets, i.e. you would use a sample. You would try to ensure, unless there was a valid reason otherwise, that your selected sample was truly representative of the population of DIY outlets. With any research the total population in question is termed the *sampling frame* and the individuals within the population are called **sampling units**. Examples of sampling frames are students in your university, all the DIY retail outlets in the UK, packets of a par-ticular brand of chocolate produced in a factory, and so on. The sampling units are, therefore, the individual students, outlets and the bars of chocolate.

Samples are useful in research. They save money and time as it is virtually impossible to investigate every sampling unit of the population. Also, because the number of units is limited, more time is available to collect more data than would be possible if a census was being conducted. If the sample is truly repre-sentative of the population it will provide an accurate indication as to what is hap-pening in the population as a whole.

Compiling the sampling frame

When using samples the production of the sampling frame is the first step. It must be as accurate and up-to-date as possible. Good starting points are local business directories if you want to identify local populations of shops, restaurants and similar services. Local authorities and trade associations sometimes produce lists of various types of companies and organizations. There are also professional mailing companies who will provide the sampling frame and lists of address labels to use in postal questionnaires etc., but these can prove expensive. It is often better to compile your own sampling frame. As mentioned previously, one of the authors (BW) carried out a survey of the manufacturing industries of East

Yorkshire and North Lincolnshire. Searching the literature located regional directories and lists containing details of the manufacturing industries – this provided the basis for the sampling frame. Good information retrieval skills were, therefore, needed at this stage of the research.

An accurate sampling frame is very important as it helps to reduce bias, and ensures that the sample used truly represents the population from which it is taken.

Methods of sampling

There are two basic ways of choosing samples: **random (probability) sampling** and **non-random (non-probability) sampling** and they are outlined below. Some of the techniques (e.g. quota sampling) are not necessarily suited to a dissertation, but an appreciation of each may help you when making a final selection.

RANDOM (PROBABILITY) SAMPLING

This works best with a very accurate and up-to-date sampling frame and is the preferred method if you intend to carry out any form of statistical analysis. With random sampling every sampling unit or member of the population has an equal chance of being selected. Each member of the sampling frame is given a number starting at 0 and the sample is selected using either random number tables or numbers generated by a calculator or computer. It is essential to realize that it is only the method of sampling that is without bias; the final sample selected may very well be biased. For example, if you were investigating some financial aspect of the European Union (EU) you would hope that the sample would represent all countries of the EU, but with random sampling it is possible for the final sample to be drawn from the same country.

There are three techniques of random sampling:

1. *Simple random sampling.* The required sample is chosen from the sampling frame by selecting the numbers as previously described. This technique is good where the sampling frame is not too large and each unit is easily accessible. The only issue you need to decide is whether to sample 'with' or 'without' replacement. If the item with the same number can be used more than once it is termed sampling 'with' replacement. This means that the data from a particular unit can be used more than once. Sampling 'without' replacement is where each item may not be used more than once, and another number (or sampling unit) is selected. From a statistical point of view, sampling without replacement is more precise and is preferred. Occasionally you may select a number above the top number of the sampling

frame, e.g. the sampling frame numbers 1–40 and you select 41. Simply disregard the number and carry on until you have the sample size you need.

2. **Systematic random sampling.** With large sampling frames simple random sampling can be difficult and awkward. A better way is to arrange the population in some sort of order, e.g. alphabetical, and then choose the nth member of the list after selecting the starting point. For example, if your population is of 100 units and you want a 20 per cent sample (i.e. 20 units), you would select every fifth item on the list once the starting point chosen by random number tables is selected. If the starting point was 2 the numbers selected from your list would be 2, 7, 12, 17, and so on until the entire sample was chosen. Systematic sampling is relatively quick to use and is preferred where large-scale sampling is needed.

3. **Stratified random sampling.** Here the population is split into layers or strata, which in reality are very different from one another. Examples of strata include gender, age groups, occupations, and income levels. If it is to be used correctly, stratified random sampling requires clear and distinct groups showing in what proportions they are present. For instance, if you were investigating the operation of a company's flexitime and how it affects its male and female employees, you would need to know the proportion of men to women in the company. Suppose the company employs 60 per cent women and 40 per cent men, the technique of sampling is as follows:

Decide on the sample size (say 300).

Divide the sample into two sub-samples with the same proportions as groups in the population (180 women and 120 men).

Select at random from within each group (stratum) the appropriate sub-sample (180 women and 120 men) to give a final sample size of 300.

Stratified sampling lessens the occurrence of one-sidedness as can be present in simple random sampling. Provided the population can be split into quite separate and distinguishable strata, stratified sampling is a very precise technique to be used.

NON-RANDOM (NON-PROBABILITY) SAMPLING

There are often situations where it is impossible to determine accurately the sampling frame. Also because of the nature of the research and dissertation, you do not need to make detailed statistical analyses. In such instances you can use what are termed non-random sampling techniques. With some qualitative research you need to sample with a definite purpose, and the approach is, therefore, subjective. Moreover, because of the nature of the work, you may be required to look at particular samples, as with a **case study**, which exhibit the characteristics you want to explore.

There are three main ways to use non-random sampling: **cluster sampling, quota sampling** and **purposive sampling**.

1. *Cluster sampling.* Within a population there often exist natural sub-groups which can be termed clusters. For instance, if you were looking at the training needs of business and management students, and the population consisted of all business and management students attending local education authority further education colleges in the UK, the colleges under one authority would make a natural cluster. With cluster sampling a sample of the clusters is chosen, and then sampling takes place within each chosen cluster. The advantage of this sort of sampling is that you do not need a complete and accurate sampling frame. You only need a complete list of the sampling units within your chosen cluster. **Cluster analysis** is non-random and it is different from stratified sampling in that the clusters are similar to one another, in this example, further education colleges.

2. *Quota sampling.* This technique is used a great deal with market research surveys, especially where street interviews are used. The population is divided into groups, e.g. gender, income level, etc. A number of interviewers is employed, and each interviewer is informed of the number of groups they have to sample and the number of people (i.e. the quota) in each group they have to interview. It is up to each interviewer to decide how to locate and organize their prescribed quotas. After the interviews all the data is collated together to form the complete sample.

   Quota sampling has a number of advantages. It is relatively quick to arrange, and there is no need for a sampling frame. From a theoretical perspective the main disadvantage is the presence of interviewer bias. There is no check on how respondents are chosen, for example, the interviewer may select only men or women, or senior citizens or anyone they think will stop and be interested in taking part. For many dissertations quota sampling is not usually a good idea. It is very time-consuming, and works best with a large population using a number of trained interviewers.

3. *Purposive sampling.* This is often called judgemental sampling, because the researcher picks the sample they think will deliver the best information in order to satisfy the research objectives in question. This method is particularly good if you are thinking of using a grounded theory approach (page 133). Under this general heading of purposive sampling, different types of sampling can be described. Where there is the need to focus on one particular and somewhat

unusual issue, there is what is termed **extreme sampling**. If you need to identify a range of topics you would then need to search out samples that could provide a variety of information, and this is **heterogeneous sampling**. Alternatively, you may need to examine one issue in detail, and then search for samples that are more or less the same. This is termed **homogeneous sampling**. Where there is the need to examine controversial and contentious issues you would select what is termed a *critical sample*. This type of sampling gives you enormous scope but, like all aspects of research, the rationale for a particular method needs to be well articulated and described.

Sample size

You may have decided that for your dissertation a systematic random sampling method is the best. You now have to decide on the sample size (the number of sampling units to take). Although this is a simple question, it is not a simple question to answer. Common sense would possibly suggest that a large sample is better than a small one, since an increase in sample size does decrease what statisticians call sampling error. However, there are instances when this is not the case. If the sampling frame consisted of very similar types of respondents, a large sample would not be needed. What is more important in this situation is the accuracy of the information collected from the sample. What guarantees accuracy is the careful design and execution of, for example, the interview schedule, and the design of the questionnaire, etc. The accuracy of the data collected is paramount. Mistakes made at the collection stage will be reflected in the analysis of the data and interfere with any final conclusions.

The sample size chosen is usually a compromise between the practical issues (e.g. time, money, etc.) and theoretical considerations involved. Statistical tables have been calculated which show the degree of precision (sampling error) which is theoretically obtainable for samples of different sizes. These are based on mathematical considerations which take into account accurate sampling frames, perfect sampling, compensation for the influence of bias, non-response, etc. For very large samples you are recommended to consult specialist statistical textbooks (see annotated bibliography, page 210). If you only have time to use small samples the following 'rule-of-thumb' normally will suffice:

1. If you are going to use any quantitative and statistical techniques decide at the start what type of data (e.g. nominal, ordinal, etc.) you are going to collect, and which test you are going to use. This in turn often dictates the sample size.

2. If the population is about 50 or less, sample the whole population if time allows. This means you carry out a census rather than a survey.

3. If you have to sample a population of 50 or more, then try for a sample of around 30 using an appropriate technique described. If you need to have a sample of less than 30, statistical tests like the Student's *t* test may be used.

4. If your sample is being divided into categories, as for example with stratified sampling, aim to have at least five sampling units in each category. For instance, if you were going to carry out a survey gauging people's preference for fruit drinks, the following layout could be used:

Fruit Juice Preference	Male	Female
Orange	5	5
Grapefruit	5	5
Tomato	5	5
Pineapple	5	5

Each cell in the table has five people, and the total sample therefore equals 40. If you decide to sub-divide the male and female groups say into age categories, for example, people above 30 and people below 30, this immediately doubles your sample size to 80. Although at first glance this might appear a simple thing to do, in practice you have doubled the amount of work. You now have to interview 80 people, as opposed to 40. This also causes an increase in travel, more time spent sorting out their responses, and so on. It is far better to keep the sample size small and manageable. Always stay in control when handling large amounts of data. Even with the use of computers and various statistical packages, data is easily lost, mislaid or wrongly entered into a program.

5. Finally, before you start always check with your supervisor or a friendly statistician that your approach is sound and mathematically correct.

Sampling and qualitative research

There is no reason why the principles of sampling should not apply equally to qualitative research when selecting individuals for observation techniques or interviews. In fact, the use of **non-probability sampling**, especially purposive sampling, is ideal with case study and action research. Purposive sampling allows for variation and enables particular choices to be made relative to a particular research situation.

Bias

When selecting samples it is important to bear in mind the concept of bias. Harper (1998) defines bias as 'allowing a particular influence to have more importance than it really warrants'. The whole purpose of sampling is to gather information about the population. Unless a special sample is needed for a particular reason, e.g. purposive sampling, you want the sample to represent the whole population, and as far as possible to have no bias.

Bias can arise because of a number of reasons:

1. *Sampling frame bias.* A poor, out-of-date and inaccurate sampling frame leads to bias. For instance, if you use a telephone directory to construct a sampling frame, you omit potential respondents who do not have a telephone or are ex-directory. Using the electoral register may miss out people who for various reasons have not registered.

2. *Researcher bias.* You the researcher may unwittingly introduce bias. You may make your questions too narrow, and as a result respondents in an interview do not have the opportunity to express themselves fully. On the other hand, your questions may be too broad and the answers so general that the final interpretations become diffuse and unfocused. If, as a young student, you are questioning someone much older than yourself, this may cause bias. The interviewee may want you to succeed and do well in your dissertation, and give you the answers they think you want to hear. In all good faith they may not be completely honest with you. In market research interviews there is interviewer bias which has already been mentioned.

3. *Non-response bias.* Non-response, especially in postal questionnaires, is always a problem and can generate considerable bias. You have no way of knowing how respondents would have answered the questions. People do not respond for a variety of reasons. Your questionnaire might look unattractive; they may have moved address, so they never received the questionnaire.

In reality, it is impossible to remove bias completely from any form of survey research. Sampling frames and respondents' opinions can change overnight. What is essential is that you recognize at the start the existence and the importance of bias and the potential influence it may have on your particular sampling and research methods.

Triangulation

The word 'triangulation' originally comes from navigational practice where a number of reference points can be used to locate an exact position. With academic research it involves the combination of different methodologies to study the same topic. As the subject is being looked at from different perspectives, this should increase the reliability and validity of any research findings. The mix of different methodologies should compensate for the weaknesses and disadvantages of each separate approach. The main problem with triangulation is that it can be costly and very time-consuming.

Triangulation is a general term, and different authors on management research give it slightly different meanings. If, for example, the same problem is studied using both qualitative and quantitative methods this is referred to as **method triangulation**. For example, with case study research, questionnaires, diaries and interviews can all be used. Comparison of the results gives far more information about the topic than if a single technique was used. If results from the different methods point to the same inferences, this in turn strengthens the overall argument and conclusion. This type of triangulation is good to use with a student dissertation. It provides you with an opportunity to use a number of different techniques. However, before you decide on the range to use, look at the strengths and weaknesses of each technique as related to your dissertation topic.

If the same method of data collection is from different sources, and over different time periods, this is often termed **data triangulation**. An example would be to follow the career paths of several managers over a number of years. As their careers developed you could question them (e.g. by interview) about how they saw their different positions, and how they achieved them. Obviously, this type of data collection is not normally suited to undergraduate work, but may be possible with certain postgraduate work.

There is also what is termed *theoretical triangulation*. Here the theory of one academic discipline is applied to a research situation within another discipline. With business and management this is very difficult to achieve. By their nature they are wide in scope, and already have their roots in separate disciplines like sociology, psychology and economics.

Finally, there is **investigator triangulation** where more than one researcher or observer record the same event at the same time. This is not normally possible with undergraduate students but it may be allowed at postgraduate level if research assistants are available.

Tips

At the end of Chapter 4 some useful tips about carrying out qualitative research are given. The tips apply equally to quantitative work – so give them a try if you think they will help.

Summary

This chapter has described the main features of quantitative research, including the concepts of sampling and triangulation. In summary, for the majority of dissertations the use of a variety of data collection techniques should be encouraged. It is essential, however, that the techniques are chosen with care and are relevant to the topic under investigation. Don't simply choose questionnaires and interviews because you like doing them and find them relatively straightforward. The final selection of techniques must relate to your overall research design, which in turn must be relevant to the aims of the research itself.

The key points included in the chapter are:

- The characteristic features of quantitative research including the various types of data.
- The techniques of conducting a survey, including the construction of questionnaires (postal, self-administered and telephone methods).
- The use of an experimental approach and the different types of experimental design.
- The importance and types of research sampling methods.
- The concept of triangulation when applied to business and management research.

6 Writing a proposal

Introduction

Before beginning a dissertation most students are required to submit an account that outlines the nature of their chosen subject and intended focus for study. This is usually termed a **research proposal** and you may be required either to complete a special form, known as a proposal form, or to write an outline of what you want to do, using a prescribed format or guideline. This chapter reviews the various aspects of preparing an acceptable proposal; it looks at what a proposal is, why it is important, the various layouts that may be used, and the characteristic features found in a good proposal. Finally, you will find four examples of undergraduate and postgraduate proposals, two acceptable and two unacceptable, with comments.

It may seem odd that we have waited until Chapter 6 to consider the writing of a proposal for the research underpinning a dissertation. This is deliberate. The writing up of a proposal isn't just a task completed when the topic for research is decided. There is a need for some careful thinking about the topic, its nature, and a number of issues around where, why, and how researching this topic might be achieved. These issues have been identified and considered in the previous five chapters.

The handling of this task, nonetheless, isn't straightforward. It reminds one of the difficulty faced when explaining to a friend what your dissertation, and more especially the research involved in the study, is actually about. Try it! In a sentence come up with what it is you are going to do for your dissertation. For example: you need a working title (which can easily become a labour of lost hours in getting it just right). Going further, try framing in no more than two or three sentences the **research intention** in a clearly written statement that outlines the purpose and basis of the research underpinning the dissertation study.

Straightforwardly at first glance, the task of entitling the proposed study simply seems to be a minor detail, but it is actually very tricky. It can become the stuff of nightmares if it is allowed to dominate the initial stages of planning. It is far better that the focus is on the idea of a purpose, and the re-framing of the research design. This helps pull the various parts of the project together in one summary. The **research statement**, in its own right, also requires a specialized kind of writing. As noted above a pro forma or at the minimum some guidance will be made available. For doctoral work, the summary can be quite long in the region of 2000 or more words in length. For undergraduate or Masters dissertations, they are normally shorter and there will be much less reference to detail of the field, e.g. reference to relevant literature. However, irrespective of level the key aspects of a research proposal remain the same.

Although the things you write down at the proposal stage are not fixed or 'carved in stone', they should reflect that you have given some serious thought to the chosen subject, and made a real attempt to explain how you intend to study it. Many students, however, consider writing a proposal a tedious and unnecessary chore. This is not the case. A thorough proposal indicates careful preparation at an early stage and, in our experience, saves a great deal of time later on. It always pays dividends. Good proposals lead to good dissertations.

Note this chapter does not consider the administrative details involved, for example, the dates for handing in proposals and the procedures they have to go through to determine whether they are approved or not. However, use these requirements as 'milestones', to map out your own 'dissertation production' timetable. Dissertation supervisors are well aware of your concerns, and give students plenty of notice. Details of the administrative arrangements about dissertations are usually available on course noticeboards, in course handbooks, and the like.

What is a proposal?

A proposal is a summary of the work you intend to do for the dissertation. It outlines the aims, methods and other features of the work. It includes a statement as to the nature and purpose of the study, together with some account of the background of the subject. In short, it summarizes exactly what you want to do in the time available. The key components of a proposal are:

- a description of the research problem;
- an account of why the problem is important;
- the review of literature relevant to the research problem;
- a summary of the proposed research methodology, including data collection and evaluation;
- an account of how the research findings will be used and/or disseminated.

Ways of presenting proposals vary, and academic institutions all have different formats and requirements. The examples given below cover most of the information required in a thorough proposal. The required length of a proposal varies.

Some universities require up to eight or nine pages, while others require no more than two. In general, the average undergraduate proposal is between four and six A4 pages in length. Postgraduate proposals tend to be more detailed and longer.

Why proposals are important and needed

In our experience many students can become intimidated at the prospect of producing a dissertation. A proposal starts the process off and makes you think carefully about what you want to do. It is an important stage in the whole dissertation process and ensures that you have thought about all the issues involved. Working through a proposal makes you think about many things at once and helps organize your thoughts in a logical manner. It gives you confidence to progress with the work. Our emphasizing the preparation and thinking before writing the proposal is all about the '**rationale**' for the research. This rationale is crucial, because it is the one place in which the researcher tries to convince their supervisor and/or external examiner that the research is worth doing. One important way to do this is by describing how the results of the research may be used. Think about the 'impact' of your research and how might it:

- Contribute new insights, ideas and knowledge and/or resolve theoretical questions in the field?
- Develop better theoretical models, explanations and knowledge synthesis in the field?
- Provide understanding and insights into the context which might influence public policy and/or professional practice?
- Affect and/or change the way people do their jobs in business, or the way people live?
- Contribute to your own thinking and learning and that of others in any relevant contexts to which the research can be applied?

In the world of commercial research detailed proposals are regarded as essential. For instance, national funding bodies will not sponsor any form of research until they have received and approved a detailed outline of what the research entails and/or purports to achieve as a basis for making a difference in any of the previously explained ways or context.

From a university's point of view dissertation proposals are essential. Most universities provide dissertation supervisors who guide and advise you. A good proposal ensures that you are allocated to a member of staff who has an interest and expertise in your chosen area. You may need to see your supervisor at an early stage in the drafting of the proposal. Be prepared for searching questions as to the feasibility and nature of your dissertation. As a result, you may be asked to revise your thoughts. All of this is designed to ensure that the final dissertation is a success. Remember:

1. The outcomes of the research process will reflect how well the rationale is established. So adopt a critical, reflective and questioning approach to the subject matter and topic.

2. Discuss your ideas with a critical friend and with your supervisor. It is worth reminding yourself that academic criticism is not a personal attack on you; it is meant to assist in refining the proposal in order to achieve a successful outcome.

The next section offers some examples of a proposal format – look particularly at the way the proposal is structured, and how the topic is set out as the focal point for an enquiry that is always systematic and rational as a research approach.

Suggested proposal layouts

The following six examples of proposal layouts include only the headings and any accompanying notes. They have been collected and adapted from a number of universities. Although some expect more detail than others, all require the student to give serious consideration to their chosen subject. Some universities provide special forms, while others give a series of headings and a suggested layout. With any proposal, never forget to include your name and course details, and the majority also require you to sign and date the proposal. Finally, don't forget to keep a copy of the proposal for yourself.

EXAMPLE 1

Name:

Course details:

Proposed title:

Proposed aims and hypothesis:

Methodology: (Describe here how you propose to test your hypothesis; carry out original primary research and employ secondary sources. When do you propose to undertake the research; does it involve work carried out in the workplace?)

Literature sources: (It would be helpful at this stage to review briefly any information you have read about your chosen topic. List the information sources you have identified to date.)

Reasons for choice of topic: (It would help if you outlined the reasons for your choice. Does it arise out of your work, general interest, seems like a good idea?, etc.)

EXAMPLE 2

Name and course:

Title of proposed dissertation:

Outline briefly the topic area including important debates and concepts.

What form will the research take? Is it pure research, applied research or action research?

Briefly explore the nature of the way you are approaching the problem.

Are you taking a qualitative or quantitative approach and how is this influencing your choice of techniques?

List with reasons the techniques you intend to use.

Are there any potential political and ethical issues involved?

List your working bibliography.

EXAMPLE 3

Give a statement of the precise area/subject that you will cover and provide a provisional title.

Aims and purpose of study.

Outline the research methods to be used and a justification for your choice.

Provide a preliminary outline of the information sources you have already identified. Briefly review them.

How does your dissertation arise out of the work already covered on your course?

What is the relationship of your dissertation to other subjects being studied on your course?

Your completed proposal should be no more than 2 sides in length.

EXAMPLE 4

Name:

Course:

Personal tutor:

Brief outline of research programme: (Include your aims, reasons for the choice and some outline of the work already carried out in the area.)

Details of interviews and other research methods you intend to use: (Include a rationale for your choice and why you have selected the identified methods.)

This is a particularly brief layout, but an account of the aims, some background literature and the selected research methods are still required.

EXAMPLE 5

Name:

Course:

The topic area: (Please give a brief discussion of the area chosen, the reasons for choosing it, its relationship to your degree and to the courses you have studied so far on your programme.)

Aims: (Please give a clear, precise statement of the problems to be analyzed in the form of a hypothesis to be tested. The aims should, therefore, state the main purpose of the research.)

Literature review: (Please give a brief review of the literature sources you have consulted so far which have a bearing on your chosen topic area and aims. List full bibliographic details of the works you have consulted.)

Methodology: (Give a brief outline of your methodology and how you intend to test your hypothesis. Give information about the type of data you expect to collect and the proposed form of analysis you will use after collection.)

EXAMPLE 6

Name of student:

Course:

Working title of dissertation:

Aims of the dissertation:

Relationship to previous work:

Proposed methodology and research techniques:

Proposed plan of work and research timetable:

Resources required: (Do you need to borrow recorders, do you need access to any particular computer software, e.g. NVivo, to analyze your results?)

Form of presentation: (It is expected that most students will produce the traditional report format dissertation. However, some students may wish to include a video, etc. as part of their final submission. Please note this now. If at a later stage you wish to change the form of your presentation, this is normally acceptable provided you inform your dissertation supervisor in plenty of time.)

Bibliography: (List in an accepted academic style, e.g. Harvard system, any references identified in your proposal.)

Characteristics of a good proposal

The six examples above illustrate a range of proposal layouts currently used on a number of business and management programmes. Let's revise the key points identified using Example 6 as this one covers all the main points. It is important to restate that a proposal is not aimed at limiting your ideas and imagination; these are essential in any academic work. It is a way of getting you to think in practical terms about how you intend to research and write your dissertation.

The key areas to include in any proposal are:

- *Name and course.* Although it seems obvious to state your name and course, students often in haste forget to include them. Certain universities also ask students to add their enrolment or registration number.
- *Title.* Dissertations must have a title. At this early stage a holding or provisional working title will usually suffice. You can decide on the exact wording when the dissertation is nearly complete. However, even at the start, aim for a title which gets over the idea of an investigation. A title which begins 'A study in ...' is normally too vague; decide whether you want to compare, collate, assess, etc. Don't worry if you end up with a long title. You are working on an academic document – you are not writing a catchy headline for a tabloid newspaper.
- *Aims.* Your earlier mind map will help here. You must identify the questions your research is intended to answer. Make them as specific as possible. Don't be afraid of having a large number of research questions. You can always reduce them at a later stage. This is where careful planning pays off. Once the work begins you may find that aims change in emphasis and in number. This can happen with any research, but what is essential is that at the start you specify, as far as possible, the precise focus of the research,

with the key concepts identified. When working on the aims attempt to give your work some originality by isolating how your research questions are different from what you already know about the subject. Ask yourself, from what you have read so far, how your overall approach is unlike that of other researchers.

- *Relationship to previous work – reviewing the literature.* At the proposal stage some attempt must be made to review the literature, especially at postgraduate level. Obviously, early on you cannot have read everything on the subject, but you should be able to list and summarize a working bibliography. A good start is to locate and read about ten recent articles that cover the main issues of the topic. An initial literature search will indicate the amount of information on your subject. It is important to know what other people have written about your topic in terms of theory, current issues and professional practice. An early literature search may help in deciding the best methodology and techniques to use. Keep details of all sources used and if they need to be written into your proposal use an accepted style (e.g. the **Harvard system**). The use of literature is so important that there is a separate chapter about it (Chapter 7).

- *Methodology and method.* This section of any proposal is vitally important; time spent working out the way in which data and information is to be collected and analyzed is never wasted. Be prepared to spend some time on this section. How you study a problem is as important as the results you collect. A balanced methodological approach using appropriate well thought-out data collection techniques will ensure the conclusions and recommendations you make at the end are more valid and credible. Results that are quickly gathered with no thought given to the methodological issues involved will make the research meaningless. If you have little knowledge and experience of the practical issues involved with research it will help if you re-read the previous chapters.

The key issues to address in the methodology section are:

- What is the overall methodological approach? Is it mixed, qualitative or quantitative? Are you going to take a special approach, such as action research, or use case studies?
- How does the approach fit in with the overall research design and what specific methods of data collection are you going to use, e.g. surveys, interviews, questionnaires, observation, etc.?
- If you propose to conduct interviews and questionnaires, how do you intend to use and select the sample?

- Is it possible to study the same problem using a combination of different approaches and techniques? Triangulation is very useful and is described on page 82.
- How do you intend to analyze and interpret your results? Will there be any statistical analysis involved?
- Remember – 'do-ability' is a 'cardinal principle' to be observed in research. Can you, at this early stage, envisage any practical limitations that could affect your data collection? Don't forget the basics like time and money. Your dissertation has to fit in with all your other commitments.

All this may sound daunting and off-putting; it's not meant to be. Once research starts, it is a very 'hands on' process and planning ahead keeps it in balance and perspective.

- ***Plan of work – time-scale.*** Not every proposal asks for this, but it may help if you can estimate how long each stage will take. Effective time management is essential. Dissertations have a deadline – a date by which they must be handed in. You need, therefore, to work backwards and estimate how long each stage will take. Don't be over-ambitious. All stages seem to take longer than originally planned, so allow for this in your early planning. Some students draw out elaborate charts to help them balance the time; anything that helps you is worthwhile.
- ***Resources required.*** As identified in Example 6, some universities require you to list any special equipment you need. Even if this is not required, some thought given to what you may need will certainly help at the planning stage. If you intend to use any computer software, be sure you know how to use it. Most dissertations have to be word-processed or typed. If you are not going to do it yourself, it is a good idea to make an early arrangement with someone who can help.
- ***Form of presentation.*** Again this was highlighted in Example 6. The general advice is that if you intend to vary from the traditional bound report format (e.g. an action research dissertation), talk it through with your dissertation or personal tutor. Universities often have regulations governing the ways in which dissertations are presented, and you must adhere to them.
- ***Bibliography.*** As identified earlier if you have to list the books and articles you have read do so in an accepted university style. Advice on this is given on page 168.

A final note. If you re-read through the proposal examples you will see variations in layout and the information needed. Some require comment on political and ethical issues, links with work carried out in other parts of the degree course, or reasons for the choice of topic. However, the overall aim of any proposal is similar in that you have to give serious thought about all the processes involved.

Examples of completed proposals

Four examples are given, two are acceptable, and two are unacceptable. All are fictitious. Examples 1 and 2 have been based on the type of proposals prepared by a third year cohort on a BA (Honours) Business Studies degree. Examples 3 and 4 have been based on dissertations produced by postgraduate students. With each example, the fictional student's work is in normal print and the authors' comments are given in italics. Read each proposal carefully – can you add further comments?

EXAMPLE 1 – This proposal is very brief and not acceptable

Title of dissertation

How 'Green' is Business Studies?

The title is too vague; as it stands it means very little. You have no idea what the dissertation is going to be about, apart from that it is something to do with business studies and the colour 'green'. If the student intends that 'green' should convey the idea of environmental issues, then this needs to be stated in the title.

Aims of the dissertation

To look at the various subjects taught under the umbrella of business studies, and re-assess them using a 'green' perspective, particularly within the subjects of economics and marketing.

The aim is too loose and ambiguous. How do the subjects quoted (economics and marketing) fit in with business studies? What is meant by a 'green' perspective?

Relationship to previous work

Broad ideas from economists like Schumacher, Galbraith, etc., from marketeers like Kotler and Saunders, and writers like Porter point to the concept of 'net national product' as investigated by the World's Bank Environment Department.

Apart from mentioning some well-known writers, little is given about the relationship between 'green' issues and the aims of the dissertation which wants to look at 'subjects taught under the umbrella of business studies'.

From what is written it would appear that the student has read very little, and hopes to succeed by quoting a few well-known names. On a technical point none of the writers have been cited in a correct academic format; publication dates are not given.

Methodology

A comparison of government and world statistics. A study of the role of marketing and how it can be 'green'. Examples of successful companies will be used as a case study.

Like the previous sections, this section is equally vague. What techniques will be used to carry out the comparison? How will marketing and its 'greenness' be studied? Which successful companies will be used, and what does the student mean by the term 'case study'? Also this is the first time marketing has been mentioned. Is this going to be a marketing dissertation?

Plan of work

By December, all research work to be completed, and writing up to be finished by Easter.

Again, this is too vague. Taking the proposal as a whole you have no idea how the work will fit in to any proposed time-scale.

Resources required

Government statistics, economic forecasts and predictions, World Bank accounts.

All these are valid sources, but publication details and how the student intends to access them are needed.

Bibliography

Schumacher – all works.

Galbraith – all works.

Porter – all works.

This section also lacks details; specific publication details are required.

Overall comments on Example 1
This is obviously a poor dissertation proposal. It appears rushed and ill-conceived, and the student has given it very little thought. It would need to be re-submitted.

EXAMPLE 2 – This proposal is acceptable

Title of dissertation

An investigation into the strategic issues adopted by certain major business corporations in order to establish permanent internal consulting services.

Immediately you know what the dissertation is all about, i.e. strategy, big business, the establishment of permanent internal consulting services. In short, the title speaks for itself.

Aims of the dissertation

An internal consulting unit within a major business corporation is one which is permanently established to provide professional consulting services to other units within the same corporation. In recent years there has been an increase in the establishment of internal consulting units. Possibly promoted by recent global business trends, more and more large business corporations are providing their own consultancy services. It is the intention of this dissertation to examine different companies' approaches to the implementation of an internal consulting group. Specifically, the dissertation intends to answer the following questions:

- Why do major groups establish internal consulting units?
- How are they implemented?
- What demand is there for the consultancy services once the units are established?
- What are the missions, objectives and benefits from the units?
- What factors govern their success or otherwise?
- How do the big companies evaluate the experiences gained from the establishment of such units?

By answering the above questions, the dissertation hopes to bring available theory and practice together and add to the growing literature in the field.

Immediately, you feel the student has a good idea about the nature of the topic, and has formulated some precise research questions to investigate it. What is missing, however, is the role and nature of big business corporations which are referred to in the aims, and also in the title.

Relationship to previous work

One of the first publications dealing with internal consulting was by Dekom (1969) where internal management consulting was described as a new management phenomenon. Over the years a number of publications (e.g. Gale, 1970;

Hoenke, 1970; Bellman, 1972; Allanson, 1985; Kubr, 1996) have developed the understanding of internal consulting. It has now become a professional, highly qualified and independent service, rather than part of a simple management service. Recent publications focus on the functional, conceptual and organizational issues of internal consulting. This dissertation will review the literature and the application of internal consulting with big business.

The student has identified a number of references, and would appear to have some knowledge of internal consulting. Again what is missing from this section is any mention of big business and how it relates to internal consulting.

Methodology

Both desk research and field research will be carried out. Desk research will focus on examining the literature. Field research will use a case study approach by identifying two or three big businesses where the role of internal consulting will be examined. At this stage the number of companies has not been identified, but it is hoped in the time available to consider at least two. Each company will be researched by carrying out interviews with selected staff, and by examining internal documents (e.g. minutes, internal reports, etc.) which are available. During my placement year I worked for a large pharmaceutical company and I have written permission from the company that I can use them in my dissertation. I intend to use semi-structured interviews as far as possible.

The student has chosen a case study approach and has identified a company which will serve as an example in the case study. Although the student has a good idea of the type of techniques they want to use, more detail could be given with respect to the selection of interviewees and the interview schedule to be used. However, overall the student knows how the data will be collected. What could have been included in this section is some account of how the data will be interpreted and analyzed.

Plan of work

July 2014	Early proposal. Research into the literature.
August – September 2014	Detailed literature search. Proposal finalized.
October – December 2014	Visit to companies. Interviews carried out. Literature search continued. Preliminary data evaluated.
January 2015	Layout of dissertation decided. Gaps in literature and data identified.

February 2015	Literature search and data collection completed.
March – April 2015	Data evaluated. First draft of dissertation completed.
May 2015	Final draft agreed with supervisor. Final draft submitted.

This is a good plan of work, and thought has been given to the various stages involved.

Resources required

The main resources required will be:

- different literature, including magazines, newspapers, reports, etc.;
- internal papers of the examined companies;
- interviews, discussions and other conversations;
- phone, fax, email;
- appropriate IT facilities.

Although the student could have given titles of the different literature sources, in the main this is a complete list of items required to complete the dissertation.

Bibliography

To save space this has not been included, but the student quoted over 20 references, each one set out according to the Harvard system. The student also divided the list into those references cited in the proposal and those which provided general background reading and informed the train of thought in the production of the dissertation.

Overall comments on Example 2

Compared with the first example, this proposal is a lot more detailed, and the student has spent far more time in putting it together. What is absent is any real mention of the companies which will be used in the case study. Also more detail could have been provided with respect to the methodology. However, this student would have been allowed to continue with the dissertation on the condition that these deficiencies were addressed, and these would be monitored by the dissertation supervisor.

EXAMPLE 3 – This proposal is brief and not acceptable

Title of dissertation

Total Quality Management (TQM) and Personal Motivation; the Work Environment

As it stands the title is too general and unfocused. It would appear that three issues are to be researched, namely TQM, personal motivation and the work environment. What is needed is some indication of how the three areas are related. Is the research going to look at how TQM can affect personal motivation in the work environment, or are personal motivation and the work environment going to be considered as factors that can influence TQM? Is a particular work environment going to be looked at (e.g. office, factory, named organization) or does the student intend to look at the work environment in a general sense? If you read the rest of this proposal, it would seem that the research is going to look at the implementation of TQM in the workplace. This important point is not apparent from the title as it stands.

Aims of the dissertation

The aims of the dissertation are:

1. To give a thorough analysis of the problems encountered when trying to motivate people.
2. To give an indication of the ways change can be facilitated.

As with the title the aims are not clearly focused. They are too vague. No mention is made of TQM and the work environment. The aims should give some indication of how these fit together. The student needs a longer list of aims, which specify in some detail exactly what is going to be investigated.

Relationship to previous work

In a lot of TQM books the technical problems that occur with the implementation of TQM are described very well (e.g. benchmarking, quality circles, etc.). However, the problems of at least 80 per cent of the companies working towards TQM are social. They encounter a lot of difficulties when trying to motivate their people to accept and incorporate new philosophies like TQM in their way of thinking and acting. This motivation is important, because without the full support of every individual involved, TQM will never yield the success the organization could make out of it.

In summary, this informs the reader that problems are encountered in some 80 per cent of companies when TQM is introduced. The problems involved are social ones and, unless they are resolved, any benefit which might accrue from TQM is limited. What is needed, and currently absent, is some review of the current literature with respect to the implementation of TQM and its effect on motivation. No mention is made of research methodologies that have been used and the ways organizations react to TQM. Although at the proposal stage the literature review may be limited, the citation of recent references would indicate that it has at least started. This proposal cites no references at all, and the statements like '80 per cent of companies' must be referenced.

Methodology

The research will be carried out as follows:

1. An analysis of occurring problems when personnel meet changes in their environment.
2. A survey of the ways personnel are motivated to adapt to changes in their environment.
3. Interviews and questionnaires will be completed with managers and production personnel in several companies introducing TQM.

It is apparent that the student has given some thought to the collection of data. Interviews and questionnaires are planned, but no mention has been made of the practicalities involved. The words 'analysis' and 'survey' have been used, but no indication has been given how they are to be carried out. It is the intention that several companies should be included, but again no note is made of how they have been identified and selected. Overall, the methodology section is too vague. Has any thought been given to the piloting of data collection methods and the subsequent analysis of any collected data? Also absent from this section is any rationale for the overall methodological approach. As several companies are supposedly involved, is a case study approach the one chosen? Is the overall approach qualitative or quantitative? These essential points need to be addressed in the methodology section of any proposal.

Plan of work

This dissertation will take four months from January to the end of April. It is proposed to write up the dissertation during April; the data being collected and analyzed within the first three months.

The student has given some thought to the processes involved and the scale of the workload. However, is one month adequate for the writing up of a dissertation? It would seem that there is a lot of work to be done in a relatively short time. The student may be well advised to look again at the whole dissertation, and perhaps limit the work to one company as opposed to several. The working out of the proposed plan of work helps identify all the jobs that need to be done. A detailed plan often indicates that the student is being over-ambitious. In such cases it is often a good idea to go back and review the aims and methodology. It is essential that the work is manageable in the allotted time.

Resources required

Government statistics, company information, research papers, appropriate reports.

This is too vague. Although all the above are valid sources, publication details are needed and how the student intends to access them is also required.

Bibliography

Key texts in TQM and motivation will be used.

As with the previous sections this is too vague and lacks detail. Full bibliographical records must be cited. No mention is made of any research literature. It is essential in a dissertation to review the current research in the chosen area.

Overall comments on Example 3

As it stands this proposal is inadequate. It lacks essential information. It is obvious that the student has made some effort and possibly has a good knowledge of the work involved, but this does not come over in the proposal. The proposal must show very clearly all your early thinking about your dissertation. This student wants to access several companies in a relatively short time. This may be over-ambitious. A better dissertation would be produced if the student concentrated on a single company adopting a case study approach. The overall advice to this student would be to review the proposal and re-write it. It needs to be more specific and detailed.

EXAMPLE 4 – This proposal is acceptable and is based on one prepared by a part-time MBA student. She was a manager in the administration department of a sports clothing manufacturer. The company's name used here is 'Sportsline' – it is purely fictitious. Note that with this type of dissertation it is essential at the start to obtain the permission of the company involved.

Title of dissertation

Flexibilization of working hours: an investigation into the factors influencing the introduction and implementation of a flexible working hours policy for the administrative staff of a clothing manufacturing company.

Although the title is long, it is self-explanatory. Immediately you know what the student has in mind. The dissertation will research flexible working hours, its introduction, its implementation. The research is focusing on one particular group of staff in one company. In short, the title speaks for itself.

Aims of the dissertation

The personnel employed in the production side of the manufacturing industry have mostly worked shifts and irregular hours. Flexible approaches to working hours (flexitime) for other workers have been on the increase in the UK in a very substantial way throughout the 1980s,1990s and 2000s. It is the intention of this dissertation to examine the flexitime policy with respect to the administrative staff of the clothing manufacturing company, 'Sportsline'. Specifically, the investigation intends to consider the following:

1. To examine the current theory of flexitime and other similar areas of time-management with respect to the manufacturing industry.

2. To identify the current models of flexitime and how they may be applicable to 'Sportsline'.

3. To identify the external factors (e.g. local government, the role of national government and EU, trade unions, professional agencies, client base, etc.) which may influence the introduction and implementation of flexitime.

4. To identify the internal factors (e.g. social implications, staff cover, sick and annual leave, travel to and from work, etc.) which may influence the introduction of flexitime to 'Sportsline'.

5. To research by surveys, interviews and questionnaires the attitude of staff before and after the introduction of flexitime.

6. To identify and assess the potential benefits and limitations of the introduction of flexitime.

7. To arrive at a suitable flexitime policy that could be introduced into the company and how this could be implemented on a day-to-day basis.

8. To provide a suitable model for the successful introduction and implementation of flexitime which could be used by other companies.

This is a comprehensive list of research objectives. Indeed, when the work actually starts it may be over-ambitious and too much to complete in time. The student may need to specialize, and could, for example, simply consider the external and internal factors that influence the introduction of a flexitime policy. These areas may be sufficient to produce the dissertation. Any unused research questions are not necessarily superfluous. The student is working in the company and remaining aims could be researched at a later date. The definition of research given earlier in Chapter 3 (page 27) included the phrase 'elucidatory comments'. Therefore, the unused aims in this example could be discussed and reviewed in the discussion and conclusion sections of the final dissertation as areas of further investigation worth doing. This indicates that any work carried out in the early stages is not necessarily wasted, and could be beneficial both to the student and to the company.

Relation to previous work

A survey conducted by Price Waterhouse (1995) looked at more than 16 000 enterprises in 17 European countries, and identified five key areas of common development. Besides pay, equal opportunities, training and trade unions, flexibility of work was one of the key areas. An early examination of the literature indicates there has been a widespread growth in atypical work patterns with a rise in temporary, part-time and other contracts. It is estimated that one-third of the current UK workforce now works a shift or similar pattern of work, including weekends and evenings. The retail industry has already recognized the need for flexibility (Klein-Blenckers, 1993). It is accepted that in retailing the workforce determines more than any other factor the success or otherwise of the organization.

Recent research (e.g. Linnenkoh and Rauschenberg, 1996; Fieldler-Winter, 1995 and Wunderer and Kuhn, 1995) reviews the implementation of flexible working patterns. Various models of flexitime have been put forward, for example, trust schemes and corehour systems, together with some account of the factors that may influence its introduction into a company. This dissertation will continue to develop this review in respect to the clothing manufacturing industry.

The student has made an excellent start and a number of research-based references, as opposed to textbooks, have been identified, However, the emphasis in part focuses on different patterns of work, e.g. shifts, rather than how time is managed at work. Also some statements are made, for example, about the UK workforce where no reference is cited to provide the back-up evidence. More specific references are needed with respect to flexitime, together with more information about its current use in the clothing industry. The aims of the research concentrate on the administrative staff, rather than the production side and senior management. This needs to be noted in the literature review. Some consideration of the research methodologies used in the literature would also be useful. Overall, however, the student has made a good start in reviewing the literature.

Methodology

The research will use a combination of documentary and empirical research. Documentary research will focus on examining the literature. Empirical research will adopt a **case study** approach and investigate the role of flexitime in the company 'Sportsline'. As a manager in the company I have access to company information, and the chief executive has already agreed that I can use the company as a case study, on condition I keep the company informed about progress on a regular basis. In addition, I am being allowed to use the company newsletter to brief and inform the administrative staff about the research. The HR department will allow me to distribute questionnaires along with monthly salary slips. All administrative staff will be invited to take part, and a sample will be chosen for interviews and the questionnaires. Information collected will be treated as confidential. If time allows it is intended to run **focus groups**. Qualitative data analysis will take place. It is realized that a case study approach is limiting in certain respects. Questionnaire and interview schedules are at the draft stage and will be piloted in the near future. An account of the organization of 'Sportsline' will be included (possibly as an appendix) to provide the contextual background to the research.

The student has begun to work out exactly how to collect data, and both the methodology and data collection techniques are in hand. More attention needs to be paid in the selection of employees, and details of sampling have to be finalized. The monthly feedback to the company could be built into the methodology. As the student is part of the company being investigated it is important that this relationship is considered. The student must try and remain as objective as possible. It could be argued that because of the student's position in the company, observation techniques would be an excellent method to use, and some attention should be given to this. It is obvious that the student has given careful thought to this part of the dissertation. The points noted in this section could be resolved after discussion with the dissertation supervisor.

Plan of work

August	Early proposal. Research into the literature.
September/October	Detailed literature search. Proposal finalized.
November/December	Data collection carried out. Literature search continued. Preliminary data analyzed.
January	Layout of dissertation decided. Gaps in literature and data identified.
February	Literature search and data collection completed.
February/March	Final data evaluation. Draft dissertation written.
April/May	Final draft agreed. Dissertation submission.

This is a good plan of work and thought has been given to the various stages involved.

Resources required

The main resources required will be:

1. Different literature including reports, papers and government publications.
2. Internal documentation of the company, 'Sportsline', including minutes and newsletters.
3. Rooms to hold interviews and focus groups. Production of questionnaires.
4. Telephone, fax and email.
5. IT facilities.

   Although the student could have given titles of the different literature sources, in the main this is a complete list of items required to complete the dissertation.

Bibliography

To save space this has not been included, but the student quoted over 18 references (mainly research-based), each one set out according to the Harvard system. The student also divided the list into those references cited in the proposal and those which provide a general background and inform the train of thought in the production of the proposal.

Overall comments on Example 4

Compared with Example 3, this proposal contains a lot more information and the student has spent far more time in putting it together. Although a number of omissions have been identified, and comments made about the dissertation, what is presented is a good start. It could even be argued that in part there is too much work here and that the student, depending on progress, may need to cut back. The student, however, would be allowed to continue with the dissertation on the condition that any deficiencies were addressed.

Summary

This chapter has focused on the importance and production of a proposal for your dissertation. They are an important stage, and as has been stressed throughout this chapter early preparation pays dividends in the long term. Take time and effort at the proposal stage – it's well worth it.

The key points included in this chapter are:

- The nature and need for proposals.
- Why proposals are required before the start of any research.
- Examples of suggested proposal layouts are given.
- The characteristic features of a good proposal are explained.
- Examples of undergraduate and postgraduate proposals are included.

7 Using the literature

Introduction

Throughout this book constant reference has been made to the importance of literature and how this can help set your dissertation in the context of what other people have done. This means you must access and evaluate as much of the published information as possible. In order to do this you need to have a good working knowledge of business and management information, the ways in which it is organized and classified, and the most effective way to retrieve and evaluate it. Information is available in many different formats such as books, periodicals and the Internet. The amount of information available is increasing all the time. Depending on the time you have to complete a dissertation, you may not be able to read every single piece of published material on your particular topic, but with care, patience and good retrieval skills you will be able to access a great deal.

This chapter is, therefore, about business and management information and the subjects covered include:

- Why you need information in the first place.
- The types of business and management information sources which are available. This includes primary sources, secondary sources and other sources. The advantages and limitations of each are discussed, with advice on how to locate them. The importance of the Internet is also discussed.
- The organization of business and management information in libraries. In order to search effectively you need a working knowledge of how libraries organize and classify their stock. Mention is made of some special libraries and how they may help you.
- Guidelines on making a literature search.
- The importance of evaluating the information. This stage is essential. The material you collect is only part of the process. How you evaluate and use it is equally important. Unfortunately, this stage is often overlooked and rushed by students to the detriment of their dissertation.

- Advice is given on how to structure the collected and evaluated material into the literature review – an essential part of any dissertation.

Why you need information in the first place

It is essential with any dissertation that you identify where your work fits in with previously published work. A knowledge of what's gone before will give you a 'state-of-the-art' background. This will help place the dissertation in its relevant context, together with any theoretical frameworks which may be involved. It may also trigger your imagination, and help you set the work in a new and different light.

In summary, you need information to:

- Ensure that your dissertation is not an unnecessary replication of work already carried out. It is perfectly acceptable to repeat a piece of similar research, but there needs to be a valid reason. For example, do you doubt the methodology used, disagree with the results, or question the theoretical underpinning of the work?
- Inform your research design and methodological approach. This may provide a foundation on which to base your chosen data collection techniques.
- Provide the appropriate contextual, theoretical and background information.
- Identify other researchers interested in the same subject area.
- Identify gaps in the knowledge about your topic. You can then speculate why there are gaps. Is it because no one has identified them before, or are the gaps, for whatever reason, somewhat difficult to research and study?
- Confirm basic ideas and knowledge about the subject while identifying redundant and out-of-date concepts.
- Identify contemporary and current thinking about the subject. You can then compare your work. A well-argued comparison is a very effective section to include in any dissertation, especially if evidence from published work confirms and supports your ideas.
- Confirm your commitment and interest in the subject.

Never underestimate the value of published work. It will form the basis of the literature review section of the final dissertation (see page 125). At the start a trawl through the literature, even using the Internet, can be a daunting exercise, but it does get easier. What you need to do is constantly revise the information you collect and see its relevance in the wider context. The key to successful literature searching is, as you go along, to re-evaluate and re-assess the material. Remember there are packages like EndNote available that can help your search and record keeping.

Types of business and management information

This section summarizes information sources which will be useful when working on your dissertation. There is a tremendous variety of information available. It includes books, articles (usually referred to as research papers), letters, committee minutes, diaries, company reports, periodicals and so on.

Information is classified into **primary material** and **secondary material**. Information which is new and original at its date of publication is termed primary material. It is up-to-date, detailed, accurate, and mostly researched based. It tends to be very specialized. Consequently, fewer people want to use it; it is expensive and sometimes difficult to trace. Because it is expensive to buy libraries only have a limited stock. Secondary material contains information which has been published before. An example of a secondary source is this textbook. The authors have used a number of different sources in its preparation. Hopefully this book has a different slant, but most of the advice it contains will be available somewhere else. Secondary material is usually less specialized and not so up-to-date. As more people want to use it, it is less expensive. It is easier to get hold of, and most libraries keep a good stock.

In preparing your dissertation you need to use both primary and secondary material. The primary sources provide details of previous and current research, while the secondary material tends to support general background and theory.

In addition, there are information sources (e.g. museums) that are neither primary nor secondary: these are described later in this chapter. They can prove useful with some types of dissertation.

Most of the references and information sources listed below are available in large academic and public libraries. An essential exercise is to find out what's available in your university. Most university libraries run workshops and offer advice on library and information retrieval skills. Make good use of what's available. Effective library skills are one of the essential attributes you need for a successful dissertation.

A useful general guide to introduce you to searching out business information is:

O'Hare, C. (2007)
Business Information Sources: A Beginner's Guide
London: Facet Publishing

Another guide is

Thompson, V. (Ed.) (2013)
Encyclopedia of Business Information Sources (2 Vol set)
London: Gale Cengage

This is available online (http://www.gale.cengage.com) and as a print edition. It includes over 30 000 sources of industry and business information. The online version has a subject catalogue of over 1 100 entries.

Finally, the amount of information is growing at an alarming rate, so you need to be aware constantly of what is available. Although the details about each source listed were accurate when this book was written, new editions are being published all the time, so do check on publication dates, etc. Details for locating each source have been included where possible.

Information and the Internet

The Internet has revolutionized the way information can be stored and retrieved. It is a research tool in its own right. Electronic versions of many well-known academic books, indexes and journals are now stored on databases and their respective websites can be accessed easily. Some journals are now only published as electronic editions.

Each Internet website has a unique address termed a uniform resource locator (URL) such as http://www.bl.uk/ – this is the Internet address for the British Library in the UK. However, although the Internet is easy to access and search, the information it contains is unstructured in terms of classification. Website pages are not classified and organized to a standard system like books in a library. The Internet is not regulated in the same way as more conventional forms of information. Anyone can place material on the net, design and launch their own websites. Everyone is free to do their own thing. As a result, vast quantities of information are available. When writing this book, for example, the authors searched sites using the subject term 'dissertation skills' and scored 100 334 hits! The amount of available information can often complicate the search procedure. What do you keep and what do you discard? The information on the net is also easy to change. Indeed, this is one of its strengths. For example, world stock market sites can be updated immediately as share prices change. However, the transient nature generates problems. An article you found yesterday may not be there today. Because the information is changed so easily how do you prove it is accurate and valid?

The Internet will save you a great deal of time, but you must take care when you begin to evaluate the material. You have to judge its quality, and whether it is suitable for your dissertation. Ask yourself some very basic questions. Where did the information come from? Is it a well-known website? Does the material look genuine? Is it well-researched and well-presented or even spelt correctly, or has it just been sent to the net without any checking? Is there any indication that a particular site has a review or editorial process to verify and check the material it holds? Information on the Internet is often pointed and biased. It may be unsubstantiated, from people whose background is unknown. Often you have no idea who the author is. It is offered with no guarantees of any sort. The evaluation of the collected material is an essential part of using the literature. It is discussed, in more detail, later in this chapter.

OTHER USES OF THE INTERNET

The Internet also provides email, bulletin boards, discussion groups, instant messaging, chat rooms, newsgroups and most recently social networking sites like Twitter and Facebook. If you use these sites you may come across someone who is researching a similar topic to you – they may even be a student working on a dissertation. This may help you refine your thoughts and generate ideas about your work. However, you often have no idea who you are linking up with so always be cautious. Remember, millions of people are using the Internet at any one time.

USEFUL WEBSITES

As stated above many well-known publications are now available on the Internet. In addition, there are dedicated websites for business and management. The following is just a small selection of those available.

> *About.com* – http://www.economics.about.com
> A good site for all aspects of economics.

> *Dow Jones* – http://www.businessdirectory.dowjones.com/
> A good source for international business matters.

> *ebusiness Forum* – http://www.ebusinessforum.com
> Produced by the Economic Intelligence Unit, UK, it contains a lot of information about e-business.

> *Mondo Search* – http://www.mondosearch.com
> This is a search engine for all corporate sites and is useful to find details about companies.

Primary and secondary sources

The following list of sources has been divided into primary and secondary. The main points about each one are explained, together with some detail about their respective advantages and limitations.

All the sources, indexes, guides and catalogues listed are well-known and should be found in most university and large public libraries. A number are published in both paper and electronic versions. Although certain Internet sites are free, many are not and you need to be a subscriber to have access. Most university and large public libraries take out subscriptions to a large number of sites. They should provide you with the necessary login details (password, username, etc.) you need to access the respective sites free of charge.

Primary sources

This includes academic journals, conference proceedings, official publications and statistics, patents and trademarks, reports, standards, theses and trade literature. These are explained as follows:

ACADEMIC JOURNALS (ALSO TERMED PERIODICALS)

These form one of the most important types of primary source to use. Most business and management research is published as articles (also called papers) in academic journals and periodicals. The range is enormous, and many are now published directly online. There are general titles (e.g. *Management Today*) and very specialized ones (e.g. *Harvard Business Review, Journal of General Management, Journal of Business Ethics,* etc.). Most academic journals have editorial boards made up of researchers and academics in the field. They referee and check the papers before they are published, so quality and accuracy are usually guaranteed. This is termed peer review. Most university libraries hold a range of titles that reflect the research interests of the lecturers and university departments. However, since such a large number are published, most universities only subscribe to a limited number.

Fortunately a number of commercial websites are available that can save time in searching out research papers. The sites are owned by various publishing companies. They are not free, but most universities subscribe to a limited number. Excellent sites for business and management are:

ABI/Inform – this is owned by the Proquest Group and has access to over 6800 management publications. Its coverage goes back to 1923. The URL is http://www.proquest.com

Business Source Premier – this is part of the EBSCO Publishing Company. The site goes back to 1965 and can access over 2 000 journals. It also contains market research reports, company profiles and industry reports. The URL is http://www.ebscohost.com

Emerald – this is part of the Emerald Group Publishing Ltd, and has information on over 2 000 journals. The URL is http://www.emeraldinsight.com

Ingenta – this also has an excellent range of business and management literature. Part of the Publishing Technology Group, the URL is http://www.ingentaconnect.com

ZETOC – this is part of the British Library, and all subjects are included. Coverage starts from 1993 and the site is updated daily. The URL is http://www.zetoc.mimas.ac.uk

A very special type of paper is the literature review, which looks at and summarizes various trends in research that have taken place over a number of years. You have to write a review in your dissertation (see page 163). A good publication which lists journals containing review articles is:

Annual Reviews
This is based in California, US. The URL is http://www.annualreview.org

CONFERENCE PROCEEDINGS

Business organizations, learned societies, academic and other associations all hold conferences (also called symposia, congresses, study groups, workshops, and colloquia). People run sessions and give talks, and most of them are published as articles (called papers) in special books called proceedings.

The information given at conferences is specialized and up-to-date. Often a new idea is presented at a conference before it appears in print somewhere else. The main problem with conference material is that it can be difficult to trace. A good place to search is the UK's British Library. They have special conference collections. Their website address is URL: http://www.bl.uk

The British Library is an excellent source to use for all types of searches. A thorough look at their website is very worthwhile.

The Web of Knowledge produced by the Thomson Reuters Organization is another good source to use. There is a dedicated Conference Proceedings Index. It covers over 23 000 conferences. The URL is http:www.wokinfo.com

The Web of Knowledge is a tremendous information source and worth using if it is available. It covers many subjects and some of its records go back over 100 years.

OFFICIAL PUBLICATIONS, INCLUDING OFFICIAL STATISTICS

Governments and organizations like the EU and United Nations produce large amounts of information that are important to all aspects of business. For example, new regulations which can influence trade between nations are being published all the time. The official publications in the UK include Acts of Parliament, command papers and departmental reports. The list is endless, and new publications appear every day. Official publications can provide information which will broaden a topic and help set a dissertation in a national and international context. They often provide a political insight into a subject. They are accurate and many include bibliographies which are also good sources of information. The main limitation with official publications is that they are written in a formal style and not easy to understand at the first reading. Most official publications are given a unique reference number; always quote these accurately when using services like the Inter-Library Loan (ILL) system. Good sources to trace official publications are as follows:

> In the UK *UKOP: Catalogue of UK Official Publications* is the place to start a search. This is available online at http://www.ukop.co.uk
> It has been published since 1980 and contains reports by UK government departments, agencies, quangos, the UN and WHO.
> The UK's National Archives at Kew, London, UK also hold copies of some official documents. All online documents can be printed out as required. The website's URL is http://www.official-documents.gov.uk
> The Archives at Kew have information on many different topics – their website is well worth a look. The URL is http://www.nationalarchives.gov.uk

If you want to trace EU information, try to find your nearest European Documentation Centre. There are over 50 in the UK and they receive every EU publication. Your university library should be able to inform you of your nearest one. They all have specialist librarians on European matters. A good site for EU material is http://www.europe.org.uk

All countries have official websites. Most search engines will direct you to a particular country.

OFFICIAL STATISTICS

In addition to producing reports, UK government departments collect data on all aspects of industrial, commercial and domestic life. These are published as official statistics, and it is possible, for example, to find out how many electric kettles were bought in the UK in 2004. It is the Office for National Statistics in Cardiff, Wales, UK which collects and collates all the data. Statistics are available in many topics (termed themes) including agriculture, population and the economy. It is possible to search the website by area, place and region in the UK.

The website's URL is http://www.ons.gov.uk

PATENTS AND TRADEMARKS

If you have a new idea which could be manufactured and sold, in order to protect it from unauthorized production, you need to obtain a patent. This is a legally enforceable monopoly granted to the inventor to prohibit others from making, selling or using the idea without permission. They are sometimes referred to as an '**intellectual property**'. They are very important in business and may be helpful with dissertations on brand names and marketing. With patents it is possible to carry out a patent analysis which looks at the number and type of patents published over several years in a particular area, e.g. pharmaceuticals. This can be used to show trends and possibly forecast the direction in which research and development should take place. Searching in this whole area can be difficult, and if you are going to do a lot of work with patents, it is worth seeking out specialist advice. In the UK it is the Intellectual Property Office that is responsible for patents. The website address is http://www.ipo.gov.uk

The Google search engine also has a patent search facility. The Intellectual Property Office can also provide information on trademarks, as can the British Library.

REPORTS (INCLUDING MARKET RESEARCH REPORTS)

Reports are an excellent, often under-used, source of information. They are published on all aspects of business and management by government departments, trade associations, academic bodies, special committees, and so on. A good source to start a search is the British Library (http://www.bl.uk)

Market research reports are very important for business. The British Library holds a large number. A good site for this type of report is that of a market research company based in the US. The URL is http://www.marketresearch.com

STANDARDS

Standards are very important in business and may be helpful if your dissertation involves the service industries. In the UK there is the British Standards Institution (BSI), founded in 1901. It is the world's first national standard body. The Institute's famous Kitemark is found on everything from power plugs to can openers. There is even a standard on the presentation and layout of dissertations! Standards come in various forms, for example, size, performance, test methods, terminology, quality management, occupational health and safety, and codes of practice. The URL of the BSI is http://www.bsigroup.co.uk

The BSI serves more than just the UK. It has more than 50 offices worldwide, and has over 65 000 clients in over 150 countries.

There is also an international organization for standards. This is the ISO (International Organization for Standardization). Based in Switzerland this is the world's largest developer of voluntary international standards, and has over 162 members. The URL is http://www.iso.org

THESES

This is one of the best places to start a literature search especially for postgraduate students, although undergraduates are encouraged to take a look as well. When postgraduate students are awarded a Doctorate degree they are required to deposit a copy of their thesis in their university library, which must be available through the ILL system. Remember the word 'thesis' is an alternative term for dissertation. As they are assessed by a panel of examiners, the quality of the work is high. If you can find a Doctorate thesis on a similar topic to yours it will certainly save time in identifying relevant literature. They are easy to trace, and are an excellent place to begin a literature search. The site to use is *Index to Theses*. The URL is http://www.theses.com

This is not a free site, but it is an excellent source, with over half a million titles in its database, with some records going back to 1716.

TRADE LITERATURE

Industry and commerce produce large quantities of information ranging from leaflets advertising new products to detailed consultancy reports. All of this is termed trade literature and can be very useful in a business dissertation. The main drawback is that the quality varies and most of it is never saved. Modern trade literature is easy to get hold of as most companies now have their own websites. Simply write or email to any company or organization you are interested in, and see what they send you.

Old trade literature is difficult to obtain, but the British Library is a good place to start. The British Library has an excellent collection of trade literature with over 12 000 items. It includes a wide range of products including electronics, agrochemicals, banking and sports equipment. A special collection in the Library is the Ettridge Collection. It was acquired in 1977 from a Mr Ian Ettridge, who worked for over 40 years in the design of domestic appliances with such brands as Hotpoint, Electrolux and Morphy Richards. The collection includes brochures, design manuals and product samples. It would be a wonderful source for anyone doing a dissertation in this area.

Secondary sources

These include bibliographies, current awareness publications, newspapers, reference books, textbooks and translations.

BIBLIOGRAPHIES

Many new books are published each year and it is very difficult to keep abreast of what is available. One way is to make regular use of commercial bibliographies. A **bibliography** is a list of publications, and for each one full details are given. Commercial bibliographies are available which can help if you need to find a general book on a new subject about which you know a little. Most academic libraries keep a number in stock. A well-known one is:

British National Bibliography
It is online through the British Library and the URL is http://www.bl.uk/ bibliographic

Another source is *British Books in Print.* The URL is http://www.booksinprint .com

Currently it has over 70 000 titles in over 61 subjects. It is not free, but comes in two editions. There is a US edition that covers the US and a global edition that lists US, Canadian, European and Australian publications.

CURRENT AWARENESS PUBLICATIONS

With such vast quantities of information being published, it is virtually impossible to keep up-to-date with every new publication. One way to help is to use current awareness publications. Commercial publishers go through all publications extracting details of subjects, authors and other publication information. This data is then re-published either in the form of indexes (publication details only), or abstract (a summary of the work plus publication details). A number, applicable to business and management, are listed below.

Indexes

There is the *British Humanities Index* This started in 1962 and is part of the Proquest group (URL http://www.proquest.com)

Current Contents is also very good and is available online and in a print edition. It is part of the Web of Knowledge (see page 112) group. The Current Contents Business Collection includes general areas of business, economics, marketing and human resource management.

Abstracts

BIDS. This is really excellent. It is the Bath Information and Data Services group. It started in 1991 and includes over 7 000 journals in all subjects. BIDS is an extremely versatile and efficient information searching tool. If it's available, then use it. It is one of the best retrieval systems on the market. You can search in a number of ways: by keywords, author, paper title and research topic. The URL is http://www.bids.co.uk

NEWSPAPERS

Newspapers are an important source of business information. They provide public and political opinion, which can be useful to broaden a dissertation. The main limitation is that they are produced at great speed and are sometimes inaccurate. They can also have a strong political bias. National newspapers in all countries have their own websites and often have access to old editions. In the UK there is the British Newspaper Archive. The URL is http://www.britishnewspaperarchive .co.uk

The website has records dating back to 1800. The site can be searched by newspaper title and specific region in the UK. It is worth a look.

REFERENCE BOOKS

No library is complete without a selection of standard reference books, such as dictionaries, directories, encyclopedias and so on. The definitive guide to reference publications is *Walford's Guide to Reference Material*. This is a 'classic' book and is readily available in nearly every UK library. *Wikipedia,* the free encyclopedia on the Internet, may be a place, depending on your topic, to get some background material, but when searching the site bear in mind the above comments about unsubstantiated material on the Internet. The URL is http://en.wikipedia.org

TEXTBOOKS

Textbooks are excellent for providing general background and theory, but a dissertation requires detailed research finding, and up-to-date detail. It is, therefore, advisable to use textbooks sparingly. Make your focus searching out primary material. Ask your supervisor to recommend a title if you need an introduction to a new subject.

TRANSLATIONS

Although English tends to be the main language of business, occasionally you may come across an article in a foreign language. In many instances important work is translated into English, and the British Library has a large number of journals in translation. Also certain search engines have translation software that may help.

Other sources of information

In addition to traditional forms of information like journals and books, there are other sources that are equally useful in business and management. These include audio-visual material, museums, information about organizations and companies, and people.

AUDIO-VISUAL MATERIAL

This includes films, videos, tapes, and CDs. Many programmes on television are about business and current affairs and these can provide excellent material for dissertations on topical issues. In addition, a number of films and videos about business issues are published commercially. The following may help you to find what is available.

BUFVC Catalogue

This is the catalogue of the British University Film and Video Council. It lists material published in all British higher education institutions. The URL is http://www.bufvc.ac.uk

There is also the British Library Sound Archive; this has a large collection of discs, tapes, films and videos. If you are investigating a particular company, the archive may hold something which could prove useful. The contact address is

Sound and Vision Archive
96 Euston Road
London
NW1 2DB
Tel. +44(0) 20 7412 7691

Museums

If you are researching changes in office layout and associated work practice, for example, a visit to a museum may prove useful. You will be able to see at first hand how the work environment has changed over the years. Museums are excellent storehouses of all types of information, but most of their stock is never put on public display. In the UK certain museums collect artefacts about dedicated subjects, for example, at Coventry there is a museum specializing in the car and motor vehicle industry. Also a number of UK local authority museums have dedicated education officers who may be able to help with a particular query. A good guide to UK museums is to contact the Museum Association. It is the oldest association of its type in the world and started out in 1889. It represents over 600 institutions. The URL is http://www/museumassociation.org

Organizations, companies and industries

Trade associations, industries, companies and other commercial organizations can provide enormous help when preparing dissertations. Most now have their own websites so access is not usually a problem. Universities have in their reference collections a number of excellent catalogues. Two good ones are:

Directory of British Associations and Associations in Ireland (20th edition)
Beckenham: CBD Research Ltd.
This lists over 7 000 associations. It is not available online, but available in print and as a CD Rom. It was first published in 1965.
Kompass Register. This is online. The URL is http://www.kompass.com

PEOPLE

People are the best information source available, and if you know someone who can help you, go and see them. Do you have friends, family members or work colleagues with business experience relevant to your dissertation subject? Obviously it will be difficult to meet well-known industrialists, politicians, etc. that you might see on television or read about in the newspapers. However, most now have their own websites and a contact email address. You can always contact them and they may reply, especially if you send a convincing account about yourself and your dissertation and why you need the information. If you want to contact a researcher or academic whose paper you have read, their addresses and emails are found either at the beginning or end of the paper. *Who's Who* is also a good source. Published since 1949 it has over 30 000 entries and is available in print and online. The URL is http://www.oup.com/whoswho

The above list is only a small fraction of what is available. In addition, maps, microfiche, science parks, information services, and news clipping services can all provide extra material. The best advice is to see what is available locally by using your university and local public library.

Libraries and business information

All libraries, even small ones, need to organize and keep accurate records of their stock. The stock is very varied, and may include books, periodicals, newspapers and audio-visual material. In recent years the role of university libraries has dramatically changed. They are now often a centre for IT and other learning support material. However, libraries still need to keep a complete record of their material and this is termed the *catalogue*. How the stock is arranged is called the *classification system*, and the exact location where all items on the same subject may be found is called the *class mark*. Libraries classify their stock using different systems. One of the first things you need is a working knowledge of how your local libraries catalogue and classify their stock. Most libraries now have their catalogue computerized, although some of their older stock may still be recorded on index cards.

Classification systems

All library classification systems divide knowledge into major areas, which in turn are sub-divided a number of times until all items on the same subject are placed together. University and public libraries use, in the main, one of two systems to classify their stock. They are the Dewey Decimal system and the Library of Congress system. Other systems also exist, e.g. the Universal Decimal System (UDS). Over the years libraries tend to adapt the systems to suit their stock and readership. The important point is that, even though you may work off campus, you must get to know how your main study libraries work and what they can offer you.

Specialized library services

Libraries offer specialized services, such as the Inter-Library Loan (ILL) service, this allows books and other items to be borrowed from other libraries. Some libraries in the UK are copyright libraries, e.g. the British Library, and by law they receive copies of everything published in the UK. Most university libraries offer services like short loan and one week loan services. Enquire what is available locally. An excellent guide to show you what is available within UK libraries is:

> *Libraries and information services in the UK and Republic of Ireland*
> *2013–2014*
> 38th Edition
> London: Facet Publishing

At the British Library there is a special business and intellectual property centre. The URL is http:www.bl.uk/bipc
> Its postal address is:

> Business and IP Centre
> 96 Euston Road
> London
> NW1 2DP
> UK

The library has also produced a series of industry guides covering 25 key industries including food, fashion, global business, green and ethical business, and social enterprise. The guides are free and can be downloaded.

Libraries in other countries

For students abroad it is important to note that most countries have national libraries which, like the British Library in London, UK, have large collections of material. If you need to use an overseas library a good source to use is the International Federation of Library Associations and Institutions. This was started in

Edinburgh, Scotland, UK in 1927, but it is now based in the National Library of the Netherlands in the Hague. Their postal address is:

IFLA
PO Box 95312
2509 CH The Hague
The Netherlands
Their email address is ifla@ifla.org
Their website address is http:www.ifla.org

Two examples of overseas national libraries are:

- The National Library of South Africa based in Pretoria.
  Their website address is http:www.nisa.ac.za
- The National Library of Israel (formerly Jewish National and University Library) based in Jerusalem.
  Their website address is http:www.nli.org.il

Guidelines on making a literature search

Having a working knowledge of the various sources available is essential if your literature searching is to be effective. As identified earlier, as you collect information, you must read it through and constantly evaluate it. The following scheme is suggested for beginning a literature search.

- *Define your topic.* Clearly define what you want to search for. Make a preliminary selection of major books and review articles. Good sources to use at this stage are indexes, abstracts, theses and reports. Use electronic versions if available as they are quicker, more detailed and easier to search.
  As far as possible, access primary sources. At this stage, have your dissertation proposal handy. In preparing the proposal you will have already begun to search the literature.
- *Decide on keyword and search terms.* Most indexes and abstracts use keyword and search terms. Decide on suitable words or terms for your dissertation. A quick mind map at this stage will help. For example, if you were searching the role of teams and team building, the search terms you look for could include the following words associated with teams: cohesion, competition, formation, ideal teams, effective teams, high performance teams, self-managing teams, team building skills, barriers to team building. If your dissertation is concerned with team building skills in relation to an IT company, you would look for examples specifically linking IT and teams. As you identify the various references, quickly scan the material to ensure it is the sort of thing you need. If not, then start again with a new set of

keywords. Effective literature searching is an iterative process and one good reference will start to lead to others. Also many papers at the start have a summary (termed an abstract). Read this first – it will often indicate whether the paper is relevant to your needs and worth reading through.

- *Identify the best sources to use.* As stated earlier, the emphasis should be on using primary sources, and as you begin to collect the sort of material you want, particular journal titles and authors will crop up a number of times. If you locate a particularly good reference, e.g. a research paper, look at the bibliography listed. This may also provide useful sources.

- *Supplement the information collected from other sources.* Once you are into the literature search, remember sources like newspapers, companies, trade associations and official publications. They can often provide an extra dimension and will give additional information to supplement the more detailed material found in research articles. Don't rely entirely on the Internet. Try and use a mixture of sources.

- *Record and evaluate the material.* Always keep meticulous records of every source used. You need these details for your dissertation's bibliography. How to set out a bibliography is described on pages 168–71. When reading the material, look for the useful quotation you may need to include when writing up. Evaluating material is very important and is explained in more detail in the next section. It is worth noting that software packages are now on the market that can take away a lot of the tedium of literature retrieval. Two well-known examples are Endnote and Refworks. Many browsers have similar facilities. Correctly used this type of software can save you time by downloading text, helping compile a bibliography and updating records. However, they cannot read the text for you. You still have to do this for yourself.

Evaluating the information

Collecting relevant information is only the first step – how you use the information is equally important. Making notes and simply summarizing the information collected and arranging it into chronological order does not constitute evaluation. You will need to identify trends, develop themes, compare one reference with another, and establish links with the accepted theories of your subject. Evaluation is really important. It is one of the most important aspects of dissertation work.

The following pointers may help you get the best from the material you collect:

- *How does the information relate to your dissertation?* Always relate the material to the objectives of your investigation. Whatever you read, be it a chapter from a book, report or article in a journal, ask yourself: 'Why am I reading this reference? Do I want a summary of the topic, or isolated examples to back up and provide evidence to support a particular point?' Never read anything without an objective in mind. Obviously when you are just beginning your literature search you will need to read most material to get yourself acquainted with the topic. However, after the very early stages, read everything with a critical and discerning eye looking for particular information – be selective! You may find that some papers repeat the same information but provide nothing new. As you read constantly search out material that is different and provides something new about your topic.

- *The basic questions you should ask.* Dissertations should be critical and analytical, not merely descriptive. This approach can start at the literature stage by asking some basic questions like 'Why?', 'What?', 'When?', 'Where?' and 'How?' about the information you collect.

- *Date and age of material.* Just because material is old does not mean it's no good. The basics may be just as valid as when first published and only the examples need to be more up-to-date. Many of the laws and principles of science still hold true today; it is the understanding and interpretation that have changed over time.

- *Primary versus secondary material.* There is a very important difference between primary and secondary material. Primary sources contain information which is new at the time of publication; secondary sources contain material which is second-hand and has been published before. For research purposes, greater reliance must be placed on primary sources. It would be unwise to base a dissertation entirely on secondary sources like textbooks. An excellent point to note would be if a secondary source has cited a primary source correctly, or has the secondary source altered the information to support a particular discussion and why? Again, read everything with a critical approach.

- *Reliance – description versus discussion and fact versus opinion.* It is essential to gauge how much you can rely on the information you collect. Ask yourself whether you are reading fact, opinion, description or discussion. This is especially important with information on the Internet. You may read that 'London is a wonderful capital city'. It is a fact that London is a capital city, but whether it is wonderful depends on your understanding and meaning of the word 'wonderful', and if you think this description applies to cities. You may well need opinion and it is a very useful exercise to include a comparison of different researchers' opinions. However, it is essential, when evaluating library material, to recognize whether what you read is based on empirical research and evidence, opinion or just a bright idea. A discussion based on this type of concept is what is looked for in a literary review.

- *Where did the author get the information from?* Very few academic writers rely entirely on their own ideas for the basis of their writing. Most use other people's work. Look at the number and type of references quoted in the material you read. An extensive and wide-ranging bibliography indicates that the writer has been thorough in searching out material. A short list may indicate a somewhat superficial look at the subject. Always go through any reference list – you may identify other useful information sources that are worth chasing up. Also who was the author writing for? Was it a general audience or other academics and researchers?

- *How did the author collect the information and is it reliable?* What type of research design, if any, was used? If the writing contains details of, for example, **experiments**, **interviews**, and **questionnaires**, ask yourself how reliable the results are. Would you believe the results of a survey based on a sample size of less than 10 people? If the author has used any quantitative methods, are the calculations correct and have **tests of significance** been used? If not why not? Academics can make mistakes like anyone else! If the researcher has used qualitative techniques, do you agree with the way the concepts and ideas have been identified as a result of the research? Do you think the researcher has made short cuts which could invalidate some of the findings? Always be prepared to ask questions. Just because a piece of research has been published in a peer reviewed journal does not mean that it can't be challenged.

- *Can you adapt, change, and repeat a methodology in either another context or with another example?* Don't be afraid to use someone else's method or approach. Provided you fully acknowledge their work it is not **plagiarism**. In fact, carrying out a piece of work, using a similar approach in a different context, may help validate both their work and yours. It strengthens the use and advantages of a particular methodology. It provides a ready-made comparison and this gives a good starting point when you come to write up your dissertation.

- *Can any published data you find be reworked to reveal new trends and new insights?* Often by reworking published data you may reveal new trends and ideas. For example, arranging a table of data into a graph or chart may help you understand it much better. It may highlight trends not immediately apparent by looking at the data itself. Descriptions of processes and long detailed accounts can often be drawn as diagrams such as flow charts. In fact, anything that helps your understanding and appreciation is useful and not to be ignored.

Structuring the literature review

The importance of the literature review has been noted a number of times in this book.

The review is an essential part of any dissertation, but it is not the easiest section to write. Unless you want a history of your topic the review is not a chronological account of all the published literature, although in many dissertations this is what most students produce. Rather, the review should be a well drafted summary reflecting the trends and significant changes that have occurred. It should highlight how your chosen topic relates to the literature and how your work adds to the body of knowledge of your chosen subject.

The following points hopefully will help you when you come to write your review. Let's recap what you have done so far. You have searched out a number of references keeping an accurate record of them. You have read them carefully and made notes, and now you are going to evaluate them. As you go through the material bear in mind the points in the preceding section on evaluation, e.g. date of publication, primary versus secondary material, the difference between fact and opinion, research methods, etc.

A good way to start the evaluation process is to ask a series of questions:

How does your work fit in with other research?
Are you adding something new and different?
Does your work agree or disagree with other researchers' results?
Does your research provide additional evidence to support a particular
  theory or viewpoint?
How has the literature influenced your methodology and data collection?
Are there any ethical issues to consider?

These are very obvious questions to ask, and you may think of more, but by answering them, and noting down the answers as you see them, you are working along the right lines. You are not just accepting the literature as it stands, but questioning it. This is an important difference. As you work through each reference in turn you will become more selective, picking out the points that relate to your work. You will begin to identify a research paper that has been well thought through before publication. You will also start to disregard material that is superficial, and adds nothing new to the argument. Chapter 9 (page 154) looks at the whole process of writing up a dissertation.

Summary

This chapter has looked at the information needs of a dissertation. It is an area that is tremendously important. Effective information retrieval and evaluation skills are essential and they should become research tools in their own right.

The key points included in this chapter are:

- Why you need information.
- The various types of business and management information sources available.
- Information and the Internet.
- The use of primary and secondary information sources.
- The use of other information sources.
- The role of libraries, and business and management information.
- Guidelines on making a literature search.
- The evaluation of published information.
- Help when writing the literature review.

8 Evaluating research results

Introduction

You have spent a great deal of effort and time collecting your research results. They may be in the form of completed questionnaires, transcripts of interviews and focus groups, diaries, or experimental data. In fact, you may have results from a whole range of research techniques. You now have to sift through and interpret them, and this forms a major part of your final dissertation. Irrespective of whether you have qualitative or quantitative results, you must relate the findings to the original aims of the dissertation. This may be a somewhat obvious point to make, but very often in dissertations the interpretation of the research evidence bears little relevance to the research question carefully set up at the start and identified in the original proposal. It is a good idea at the interpretation stage to keep a copy of the proposal handy. It is essential to recollect whether the data is quantitative or qualitative, as this will govern aspects of the analysis. Table 8.1 summarizes the essential differences between quantitative and qualitative data.

It is helpful at this stage to review the research approach and methods, and revise why they were selected. What were their relative advantages and limitations? How did the literature inform your research design? Were any special concepts and ideas identified in the literature and, if so, can they be used at this interpretation stage?

This chapter offers suggestions on how to analyze and interpret your research results. Sections are devoted to quantitative and qualitative research. There are, however, a number of general points which apply equally to both approaches and these are explained first.

General points about the interpretation of research results

Research produces a lot of results and, as they stand, they can be unwieldy, so you need to reduce the amount of material collected. The reduction of data is

Table 8.1 Comparison of quantitative and qualitative data

Quantitative data	Qualitative data
Based on meanings derived from numbers. The data may be nominal (categorical), ordinal, interval or ratio.	Meaning is expressed in words.
Collection of data is numerical and in standardized form.	Collection of data is non-standardized and uses a variety of formats.
Analysis is by the use of tables, diagrams and statistical methods. The methods used depend on whether the data is nominal (categorical), ordinal, interval or ratio.	Analysis is via the use of descriptions and the identification of concepts.

important in the process of interpretation. It must be done, however, without losing sense or order. Techniques such as tables, figures, flow charts, the listing of categories, the identification of themes and ideas all help to cut down the amount of paper and material you are handling.

As you reduce the amount of paper, look for themes, ideas and concepts which may emerge. Try to identify overarching and broad propositions which may join a number of ideas together. Are they linked in any special way? Are particular relationships emerging? As you work through the data try to separate it into its component parts. Look for reasons to explain the results.

Don't ignore the literature review at this stage. It can provide useful clues. Is your data, for example, similar to that which other people have produced before? Do your ideas agree or disagree with those of other researchers? Try and build what some people term 'conceptual frameworks'.

When working through the results constantly refer back to the way you collected them. These two factors are intrinsically linked. Have your chosen techniques proven successful and the most suitable? With hindsight would you repeat the work in exactly the same way, or make changes? A critique of your **methodology** in the light of the results is important. Research is not just about collecting results; the appropriateness of how you collected them is just as important. Be reflective during the whole process of data interpretation. Self-reflection is an important aspect of contemporary management research. It helps to establish your views and opinions about the topic, and whether or not they have changed during the duration of the research.

Guard against simply summarizing and providing a précis of your results. Without thinking, many researchers describe their results, assuming that description equates to interpretation. It does not. Interpretation shows how your results fit, or do not fit, with the theory and background of the subject investigated. Don't be afraid to challenge and question accepted practice. If your methodology and techniques have a strong **rationale** and indicate a particular line of argument, then be bold and say so. It is the strength of your argument that is important.

Finally, there is no standard approach to analyzing research results. This distinguishes research, especially in such broad areas as business and management. Don't be afraid to look for something new and different. A good and analytical interpretation will make your work stand out.

Qualitative data analysis

Gathering data should always be guided by a purpose. Analyzing any kind of data is carried out to generate a result. It is likely that your own research is linked to exploring some aspect of business and/or management. The importance of establishing both meaning and understanding is the key to good data analysis that is intended to produce, in turn, research that scores high for relevance and utility. For example, in an increasingly complex world, the effect of technology-driven application of data-smart management of information within organizations, is creating an increasing emphasis on management informed by quantitative data. The dangers in this approach are the absence of further consideration of meaning and the use of data and information as a basis for an understanding of how knowledge functions within an organization in organizational management (Sandberg and Targama, 2007). This illustrates both why and how the qualitative paradigm remains a major part of business and management research. It is also why increasing use of a multi-method approach (i.e. **mixed methodology**) is now made in research design.

Analysis is something that is rarely defined in the literature – the focus being more on 'how' rather than 'what' – but as Oliver (2012) says, 'it is an implicit part of the research process'. A useful summary of the processes that qualitative data analysis generally include are reflected in the following steps:

- grouping together of data into categories;
- allocation of names to those categories to develop new research concepts;
- exploration of possible relationships between groups of data;
- search for possible causes for observed events;
- comparison of data from different contexts;
- use of data to test a hypothesis;
- creation and explanation of a new theory.

The process of data analysis is dependent upon several things, e.g. the amount of data that has been collected; the amount of time available for analysis (it always takes longer than initially planned); and of course personal choice plays an important role. Data analysis can either be done by hand, or using software such as Word or through the use of more sophisticated computer assisted qualitative data analysis systems (CAQDAS).

Analysis can also follow several particular approaches reflecting levels of pre-determined parameters that control the scope of an analysis. This aspect to analysis is usefully thought of as creating a framework for the analysis. It is much like a garden sieve with the size of the griddle (grid) determining the nature of the soil (data) left caught in the sieve. A specific example of an approach that reverses adopting a traditional **hypothesis** or research question is 'grounded theory'. The approach is dealt with more fully later in this chapter.

It is worth repeating that qualitative research always generates lots of material. At this point of data analysis, the data has to be gone through and some sense made of it all. Although you were advised at the collection stage to think about the processes of interpretation, in reality this is difficult to do. At the end there always seems a large bulk of material to interpret.

The following practical approach to the analysis of qualitative data is suggested:

- Read through all result formats, e.g. interview transcripts, questionnaires, observation sheets, etc. As you work through, carefully note down any points and ideas that are identified.
- Go through each different type of format a second time and identify in each one what you consider to be the definitive list of ideas and topics mentioned. Give each discrete topic a code, e.g. a number or letter, so it can be identified at a later date. The overall aim is to end up with, for example in an interview transcript, the format marked up with different letters and numbers, each one representing a separate idea. Don't forget to write down what each number or letter stands for. For instance, if the dissertation was on decision-making, you might identify from your interviews the following ideas, each of which could be given a code as follows:

Idea	*Code*
Team work in decision-making	D1
Explanation of a good decision	D2
Explanation of a bad decision	D3
How to make decisions	D4
Conditions necessary to make effective decisions	D5

- As you work through your material, you may decide to include extra categories. For instance, with the above example you may begin to identify behavioural aspects of decision-making and this in turn may be sub-divided into subjects like attitude, emotions, gender, intuition, etc. It is essential that you constantly reflect back to check that ideas have not been missed. Some people, at this stage, actually cut up the interview transcript and sort each idea into individual files. This can be done on the computer, either as a word processing exercise or using a piece of software specifically designed for qualitative analysis.

- If you decide to separate chunks of data in this way, give each separate piece its own identification number, so that if you need to you can reassemble them back into their original format. Depending on how many pieces you have, making a copy of each stage is good practice. As you work through the material you may come across useful quotes given by your interviewees or respondents, which seem to summarize an idea that you have identified. Keep a special note of these. When writing up, a succinct quote used at an appropriate point will certainly hammer home your line of argument.

- Finally, when all the results have been assigned to a particular category, you then need to go back and re-read all the comments with respect to one idea. This is the stage when patterns begin to emerge and the real interpretation begins. You may be able to link some of the ideas with those already identified in the literature. It may be possible to convert some of the qualitative data into a quantitative format. For example, can you calculate the percentage frequency of a particular idea, and give an estimate of its occurrence?

The above method of analysis takes considerable time, and you need to be meticulous so that you can re-trace your steps if required. In summary, you have accomplished two things:

- You have gone through all your results and data collection records and divided them up into representative categories and ideas.
- By doing this you have identified how these can be linked to form larger and more general themes. You have begun the process of conceptualization.

Using computer assisted qualitative data analysis software

If you consider using CAQDAS remember it is a tool. It is a means to an end and it is not an end in itself. Ask yourself before you start: is it the right tool for the job?

There are several advantages in the use of CAQDAS. These include the speed with which data analysis can be completed, and the capacity to handle large quantities of data. It provides a better basis for claims on the part of the researcher to impartiality, since there is rigour and transparency in the analytical process. It arguably produces results that are more replicable (Hwang, 2008). That said, the criticism of researcher objectivity as well as the supposed lack of rigour (Baugh, Hallcom and Harris, 2010) can still be made, as choice of themes and sub-codes which form part of the data input to these systems are still dependent upon researcher choice and as such remain a subjective decision.

There are a number of popular software packages that can be used for data analysis, e.g. HyperResearch, NVivo, ATLAS.ti, Ethnograph or MAXQDA. The package you choose will depend on a range of issues including the kind of computer you have, what you want the package to do and, importantly, the level of technical support that there is available. The most popular package is NVivo. You will find courses in using NVivo online are offered by many universities, and there may be top-up classes available.

An example of the first is the website of QSR International, the owners and developers of NVivo and at: http://www.qsrinternational.com. Another very useful website offering advice is: http://www.surrey.ac.uk/sociology/research/research centres/caqdas/. An alternative and more recently developed package is called 'dedoose', and is very useful in managing data in a mixed methodological research project [see http://www.dedoose.com].

Although using these software packages can make the handling of data easier and faster, it is important to remember that the software will not do the analysis for you (Macmillan and Koenig, 2004). It is after all, a tool to facilitate data analysis. As a final thought, no matter what package is finally chosen as Basit (2003) observes: 'The computer and the text analysis packages do not do the analysis for the researcher. The user must still create the categories, do segmenting and coding, and decide what to retrieve and collate.' It is crucial that if CAQDAS software is used in the analysis of data, it is always an integral part of the research design. It should be regarded as a means to an end and is, therefore, used as a tool. It is not the 'wow' factor as identified by Richards (2002) and should not be allowed to take over and become a *research fetish* (Garcia-Horta & Guerra-Ramos, 2009).

A useful book about software and qualitative research is that by Lewins and Silver (2007).

The above approach is a general, practical description of an approach to qualitative data analysis. It should suit most undergraduate and Masters dissertations, although it is more likely that postgraduate research will include the use of CAQDAS. There are, also, some special techniques of qualitative data analysis. These include, for example, *content analysis,* where the frequency of keywords and concepts is calculated. It is really a more sophisticated version of what has been described here. Another technique uses the concept of *grounded theory,* and this is now described.

The role of grounded theory

The idea of grounded theory was presented first by Glaser and Strauss (1967). It has since spread to all areas of qualitative research, and is generally associated as an outcome of inductive research. It is theory that arises from the data collected by empirical research. A great deal has been written about it, and in many cases the original ideas of Glaser and Strauss have become altered. An excellent summary of their work is given in Denscombe (2010). The essential points about grounded theory are as follows.

Grounded theory presumes that the data is first collected through a variety of methods and then a systematic extrapolation of the data is expected to generate a theory. It is in the main a pragmatic approach. Qualitative research can be very different in that at the start no observable patterns in the data may be apparent. A prescribed approach can be too counter-productive, failing to take onboard all the complexities of what qualitative research is; it is in essence a descriptive process.

Qualitative research, it is argued, should not however, simply describe a situation, but look for explanations and analyses, and at all levels a search should be made for generalizations or theories to explain and understand the topic being investigated. These generalizations or theories should, therefore, emerge or be 'grounded' in the empirical research. Hence the term 'grounded theory'. Implicit in the process is that the researcher constantly looks back and reflects, and as a result refines the theory against new research findings.

With grounded theory the researcher must have an open mind right from the start. Pre-conceived ideas about a situation should be ignored. It is here that a problem arises. It is very difficult for any researcher to put aside thoughts about a subject. It is important to emphasize that an open mind does not equate to an empty one. If you intend to take a grounded theory approach, the literature still needs reviewing, and a working knowledge of the topic being investigated is required. The approach is grounded in the collecting of data, not the original **research intention**. The stated purpose of the research is still 'first base' and must be used as a reference point throughout the entire research project.

The following is a suggested grounded theory scheme of analysis. It is similar to the scheme already described to analyze qualitative data, in that patterns and themes are identified. The difference is that with a grounded theory approach you treat the material as a whole (i.e. holistically) while attempting to explore the meaning and context of the data. The suggested scheme is:

- *Familiarization with material.* Here you read and re-read the work, teasing out patterns and themes. In particular, search for nuances and attitudes, and get a feel for the material.
- *Reflection.* At this stage you ask questions such as 'Does the research data support existing knowledge?', 'Does it challenge existing knowledge?', 'Does it answer previously unanswered questions?', and 'If the data is different, why is it different?'
- *Conceptualization.* Here you identify patterns and concepts that begin to emerge from the data. As in the method described above, the use of letters and numbers to code material may help.
- *Cataloguing concepts.* The identified concepts are now recorded on index cards (or computer database). Each entry contains full details of where the same concept occurs.
- *Linking.* The ideas are now linked together and hopefully you start to build the grounded theory. At this stage areas may be identified where there is a shortage of material, so you may need to revisit your original data to ensure that no important point is missed, or you may decide to collect more data should the time allow.

The use of grounded theory is popular in certain areas of human resource management and in investigations that look at the cultural concepts of an organization.

Overall, any analysis of qualitative data involves searching for and revealing patterns of data which describe an identified situation or setting. As with all research, qualitative data analysis must be credible. As a researcher, you need to make sure that the techniques and methods used reflect an integrity, validity and accuracy in the findings. You need to make sure that there is consistency and clarity in the linkage between research intention and the methodology underpinning the research study.

Quantitative data analysis

In many ways the analysis and interpretation of quantitative data is similar to that of qualitative data. The same principles apply, in that the data must be reduced in bulk to make it more manageable. What concerns many students with quantitative data is the use of statistics and the associated mathematical formulae involved. Fortunately, there are now software packages (e.g. IBM SPSS Statistics, Minitab) available to lessen the mathematical burden. If you are going to use such packages be sure you understand the principles involved and what the final calculated figures actually mean. It is important to note that using statistics does not always imply long and complicated calculations.

This section works through a number of different areas associated with the handling of quantitative results. It looks at the preparation of data for analysis, which sometimes includes what is called **coding**, and the use of both **descriptive** and **inferential statistics**.

Descriptive statistics involves describing and displaying results in the form of tables and diagrams, such as bar and pie charts. Arithmetical calculations are part of descriptive statistics. They are usually straightforward and measure the **dispersion** (i.e. the spread of a **distribution**) of the data. Inferential statistics are more mathematically demanding. They involve the concept of **probability**, and the carrying out of mathematical tests of statistical significance.

An understanding of the basics involved in statistics is needed; this will help you appreciate which type to use in different research situations. It is important to think about the use of statistics at the start of your research. When used correctly, statistics are a useful research tool. However, when wrongly applied, they only weaken results and can present a misleading picture of the research.

This section aims to provide an overview on the use of statistics. Detailed mathematical formulae are not given; the annotated bibliography (page 210) lists useful books should you want more detail.

Preparing quantitative data for analysis

Quantitative analysis requires the data to be in the form of numbers. This is an obvious statement to make, but if you decide to use any type of quantitative data collection you need to think at the start how the data, if not collected in number form, can at the end be transposed into numbers. With interviews and questionnaires, for example, the collected information is mostly in the form of descriptions, or ticks in boxes. You need to transpose these into numbers. This is called *coding*. It is achieved by working through the interview transcripts, questionnaires, etc. and allocating each separate idea or concept identified a numerical code. Use the **pilot study** carried out early in the research to decide on the form of coding. This can save a great deal of time later on.

Let's take an example of coding. Suppose you are carrying out a survey of senior managers about business process re-engineering, and are using a questionnaire as the main method of collecting data. The first question might read as follows:

Before receiving this questionnaire were you already aware of business process re-engineering?

Please tick appropriate box

Yes	0
No	1

The response 'Yes' is given the numerical value of 0, and 'No' is given the numerical value of 1. When you have received all the returned questionnaires, go through the replies and count the total number of 0s and the total number of 1s. You can then go on to calculate the percentage frequencies. The above question is termed a **closed question**, in that only one type of response can be recorded, either 'Yes' or 'No'.

Some questions can be described as partly open, in that the respondents are given a range of potential answers. For example:

Where did you first hear about business process re-engineering?

Radio	[0]
TV	[1]
Newspaper	[2]
Trade journal	[3]
Other source(s)	[4]
Don't know	[5]

Please tick appropriate box
If you have ticked other source(s) please state source(s)

_____

_____

Under the heading 'other sources' the respondent could state, for example, conference, meeting with colleagues, the Internet, or attending a training programme. You need to work through all the returned questionnaires and list all the different sources identified and code them, e.g. conference would be 6, meeting with colleagues 7, the Internet 8, attending a training programme 9, and so on. As with the first example you could calculate percentage frequencies, etc.

Coding completely open questions is more difficult and time-consuming. Using the business process re-engineering example, an open question might read 'What factors govern the success or otherwise of business process re-engineering?' To answer a question like this respondents have to list their perceived reasons, and may write one or two sentences explaining their views. Here you need to work through each questionnaire, looking for discrete comments made by the respondents. Having identified all the possible replies you then code them, with the first concept being 0 and so on until every separate idea has a number. Coding open questions reflects the judgement of the researcher. In the early stages try to use as many categories of response as possible. The number can always be reduced at a later stage, and what at first might appear separate categories can be linked under the same number.

Coding is a tedious and time-consuming business and you need to double-check, particularly with open questions, that you are being consistent and applying the correct codes. Often respondents may express the same idea, but use different words. It is important that every type of code is independent and mutually exclusive of one another. As stated earlier, it is a good idea to sort the coding out at the pilot stage, and then the questionnaires can often be coded (i.e. precoded) before they are distributed.

Quantitative analysis and computers

As mentioned earlier very sophisticated and powerful software packages are now available. The majority of them are written to provide a number of functions, and once the data is input, a number of different tests and calculations can be made. They will set out and draw tables, graphs and charts. Some packages even allow for missing values and unanswered questions on a questionnaire. As with any package, practise with your pilot data.

Descriptive statistics

Diagrams and tables are an excellent way to describe and compare data. For instance, a table can augment and summarize an account of a survey, a well-labelled flow chart can be used to clarify and add to a description of an industrial process. General advice about the use of tables and diagrams is given. This is followed with a range of examples.

- In text the tables are referred to as tables, and diagrams like charts and graphs are collectively called figures. Both are numbered using Arabic numbers, and the numbers should correspond to those given in the text. The numbering should incorporate the section of the dissertation where the table or figure is found (e.g. Figure 3.4 is the fourth figure in Chapter 3). This is the system used in this book.

- Tables and figures should always be large and neatly produced, whether drawn by hand or computer. They should be given a self-explanatory title, and if you are using someone else's material, they should be referenced as with any other cited information.
- When using numbers always state the units. Big numbers can be shortened, e.g. 18 000 000 can be shown as 1.8×10^7. If levels of statistical significance are used they must either be incorporated in the title or given as a footnote.
- Don't overcrowd a table with too much information, as it will be less easy to read.
- Don't let tables and figures stand alone. Do refer to them in the writing summarizing the main points for the reader. Good figures and tables add to the written text, they do not replace it. Many students produce excellent figures and tables and only superficially refer to them in the text.

Tables

Tables are usually used to display numbers and since they are arranged in columns and rows the numbers can be easily compared: this will help to reveal trends and patterns. As actual numbers are quoted tables are more precise than figures, and the reader can identify particular values. Table 8.2 is an example of a table using numbers. It is a fictitious example, but serves to illustrate the point.

Table 8.2   Percentage of new enterprises that have sought professional 'start up' advice from management and business consultants (n = 84)

Type of new enterprise	Help needed from management and business consultants (%)
'Pop up' stores	5
Traditional markets	15
Farmers' markets	10
Antique fairs	18
Market gardens and nurseries	20
Artists' co-operatives	30
Home workers e.g. small food producers	2

Source: various

Table 8.3 The most important aspects of customer service as identified by the managers of various departments in the 'Dissertation Department Store'

Department	The most important aspect
Clothing – menswear/ladies wear	Good service
Sports goods	Wide choice of manufacturers
Furniture and household goods	Quality products
Children's wear	Staff expertise
Coffee bar	Cleanliness
Restaurant	Excellent quality
Electrical goods	Competitive prices
Cosmetics and perfume	Latest and up-to-date products

Source: various

There are also non-numerical tables, and Table 8.3 is an example. Again it is fictitious, but it represents the sort of information that might be obtained if heads of various departments in an organization were questioned about one important aspect of their work.

Figures

Figures are not as precise as tables, but do have more visual impact and are an excellent means of illustrating data. The following selection gives some idea of the range of techniques that can be used to display information in figure format. The list is by no means complete and it is worth keeping your eye open for recent publications to see if data is displayed in a different way. In the UK *The Financial Times* and *Which* both present data in novel and interesting ways. A point to note is that some figures like graphs and histograms have certain mathematical properties, so only use them if you understand the theory involved.

Graphs

A graph is an excellent way to illustrate the relationship between two sets of results (known as variables). The line drawn on the graph represents this relationship. It indicates how a change in one relates to a change in the other. Figure 8.1 is an example of a graph and shows the relationship between the number of sales in 'The Dissertation Department Store' over time. The horizontal axis of

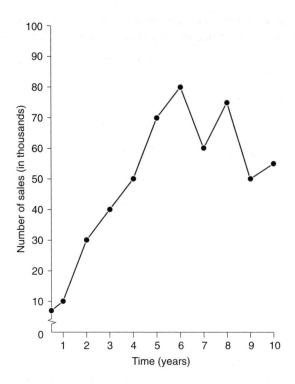

Figure 8.1 Graph showing number of sales in the dissertation department store over a 10-year period

Note: The y axis (the dependent variable) has been broken with a zigzag line because of the magnitude of the scale.

the graph is termed the **x axis** (the **abscissa**) and the vertical axis is termed the **y axis** (the **ordinate**). The **independent variable** is plotted on the horizontal axis, which in this example is time, and the **dependent variable** on the vertical axis, here the number of purchasers. The axes should always start at 0 and this is termed the origin of the graph. In most examples time is the independent variable, but not in every case. A clue in recognizing the two variables is to examine the results being plotted. The independent variable changes at regular intervals, while the dependent variable is more erratic and irregular. Figure 8.2 shows the various parts of the graph.

Many software packages now construct graphs. However, when constructing a graph always use a sensible scale for both axes. Excessive manipulation of data can make the graph look strange and is often misleading. The vertical axis must always start at 0, so if the dependent scale is long it is permissible to break the axis by a zigzag line. It is also possible to plot several lines on one graph. In

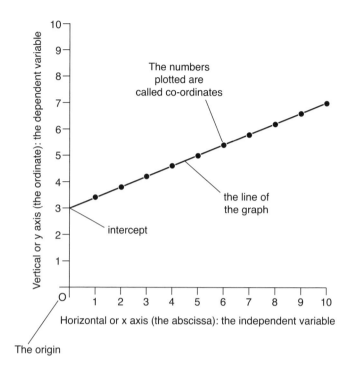

Figure 8.2 Diagram showing the various parts of a graph

Note: Scales and units on both axes are arbitrary.
Source: Adapted from White (1991)

Figure 8.1, two lines could have been plotted, one representing male shoppers, the other female shoppers. This then may show differences between the shopping habits of women and men.

As stated above, graphs have mathematical properties, and it is possible in certain situations to transpose the data and plot a different type of graph. An example is the **semi-log graph**. Here the results for the dependent variable (y axis) are plotted as log numbers, while the results for the independent variable (x axis) are left unchanged. This results in a semi-log graph, and these can be useful to compare rates of sales of two similar products.

Other graphs used in business are the **Z chart** and **Lorenz curves**. The Z chart is a graph that represents only one year's data, and incorporates within it monthly totals (again of a particular product), monthly cumulated figures for the year and a moving annual total. The graph is called a Z chart because when all the numbers are graphed they look like the letter Z. Lorenz curves are very specialized, and used to show inequality. For example, it is usually accepted that in every country a small portion of the population owns and controls a large proportion of the wealth. Lorenz curves may be used, therefore, in situations where the incomes present in the population are being studied and industrial output and efficiency are also being measured. Graphs can become mathematically complicated. Only take them as far as you understand them.

Pie charts

Pie charts are easily understood by the reader, and simple to construct. White (1991) gives instructions on how to do it by hand if you don't have a software package available. The word 'pie' comes from the fact that a circle is divided up into slices, like a cake or pie. The whole circle represents the whole sample and it is divided according to the size of each component part. Pie charts can be used as an alternative to **bar charts** and there are a number of variations in their construction. It is possible to combine the pie chart with the percentage bar chart, if one sector of the pie is especially interesting. Figure 8.3 shows a number of different pie chart layouts all using the same data taken from Table 8.4. Don't divide the chart into too many sectors: four or five is usually enough.

Bar charts

Bar charts are like graphs in that they have data on two axes, but on one axis the variable is non-numerical. Figure 8.4 shows a range of different bar chart formats, all using data from Table 8.4. This same data was also used in the pie chart examples.

Histograms

These are not bar charts, but specialized diagrams to show frequency distributions. If we take the same 200 customers at 'The Dissertation Department Store', but this time record in km how far they have travelled to the store, the distribution would be as set out in Table 8.5.

When drawn out in the form of a chart, as in Figure 8.5, the data is termed a **histogram**. It is important to note that histograms have mathematical properties, in that the area of each column is proportional to the frequency of each class. This means if one class has a frequency twice that of another, then the area of the respective column will also be twice as much. It is important to note that a histogram plots data that is continuous. In the example given, people can travel any distance to arrive at the shop. Therefore, when drawing out the histogram all the blocks touch one another. Frequency distributions which plot **discrete data** are called **column graphs**.

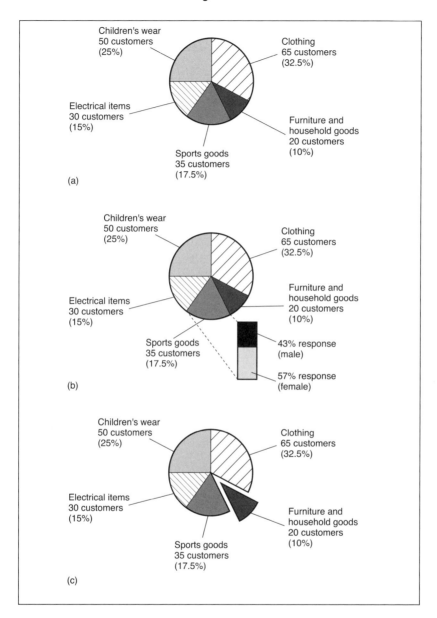

Figure 8.3 Different examples of pie chart layouts using data from Table 8.4

(a) Standard pie chart.

(b) With this layout a percentage bar chart is added to one sector to show the ratio of male to female customers.

(c) With this layout one sector has been pulled away from the pie. This is useful if you want to emphasize one particular sector.

Table 8.4   First purchase by a random sample of 200 customers in the dissertation department store on 1 January 2013

Department	Male	Female	Total
Clothing	20	45	65
Children's wear	20	30	50
Furniture and household goods	10	10	20
Sports goods	15	20	35
Electrical items	18	12	30
Total number in sample			**200**

Column graphs

If we look at our dissertation store data once again, but this time asks the customers how many times they have visited the shop in the previous six months, the data might be as set out in Table 8.6. Note that the data is discrete, because people can only enter a shop a definite number of times, e.g. 5 times or 6 times, not 5.1 or 5.2 or 5.3 times.

Figure 8.6 illustrates the data when drawn as a column graph. Because the data is discrete, each column is kept separate.

Isotypes (also termed pictographs)

This method of displaying data is very eye catching and extremely effective. In an isotype diagram the symbols used represent the subjects. For example, suppose a book shop wanted to display the number of books sold in a 5-year period, the results could look like Figure 8.7. Isotypes are interesting to look at and make a useful change. The main difficulty is finding a symbol that looks like the subject it represents. They need to be simple, easy to copy and instantly recognizable. Each symbol stands for a certain number. In Figure 8.7 ⬚ each represents 1 000 books, and half a symbol ⬚ represents 500 books. Obviously isotypes cannot be used in every situation, and it is difficult to divide some symbols up accurately to represent very small numbers such as 3, 4 or 5.

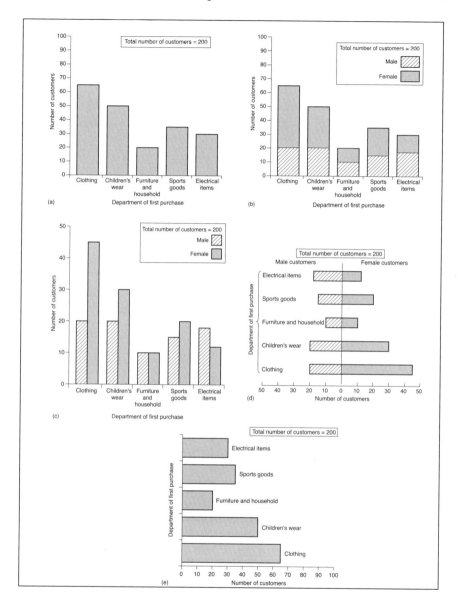

Figure 8.4 Different examples of bar chart layouts using data from Table 8.4

(a) A vertical bar chart.

(b) A component bar chart.

(c) A multiple bar chart.

(d) A back to back (or change) bar chart.

(e) A horizontal bar chart. This is useful if a large number of bars are needed; it is easy to extend the vertical scale.

Table 8.5 Distances travelled in km by 200 customers visiting the dissertation department store

Number of km travelled to reach the store	Number of customers
0 – under 5	10
5 – under 10	45
10 – under 15	70
15 – under 20	55
20 – under 25	14
25 – under 30	6
Total number of customers	**200**

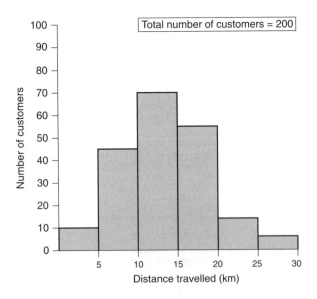

Figure 8.5 An example of a histogram showing the frequency of customers and the distance travelled to the dissertation department store (based on data in Table 8.5)

Inferential statistics

Descriptive statistics are used to describe the data you collect. The pie chart (Figure 8.3) illustrates percentages in the different sectors of the sample. What the pie chart does not indicate is whether the percentages plotted in each sector

Table 8.6 Number of times the 200 customers visiting the dissertation department store entered the store in the previous 6 months

Number of visits made to the store	Number of customers
1	10
2	18
3	40
4	40
5	60
6	20
7	5
8	6
9	1
Total number of customers	**200**

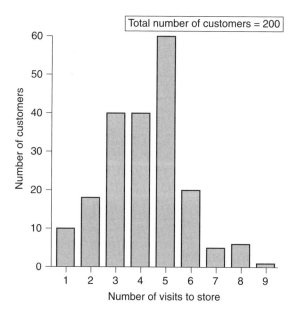

Figure 8.6 An example of a column graph showing the number of visits made by 200 customers to the dissertation department store (based on data in Table 8.6)

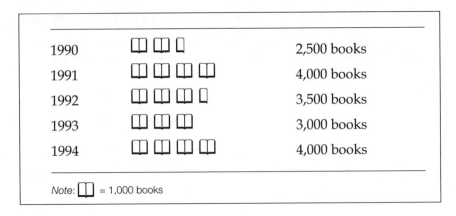

1990		2,500 books
1991		4,000 books
1992		3,500 books
1993		3,000 books
1994		4,000 books

Note: ☐ = 1,000 books

Figure 8.7 Number of books sold by a bookshop over the 5-year period from 1990 to 1994

are different because this represents the true situation and the shopping habits of customers, or whether they occurred just by chance alone on the day the survey was carried out. There is a special branch of statistics called inferential statistics which allows you to do this. Over the years statisticians have applied mathematical theory and have developed a range of procedures which, if followed, give a good indication whether the quantitative results of any investigation have arisen by chance alone or indicate that true differences exist.

This chapter does not work through all the procedures in detail, since a number of excellent books are available (see annotated bibliography, page 210). Instead, some of the main principles are explained, so if you need to use any statistical test you will have some idea what to look for and have confidence that you have selected the correct one. It has been stressed before, if you intend to use any statistical test it is essential to decide, at the start of any data collection techniques, which tests you intend to use. This is because certain tests only work with certain types of data, e.g. nominal, ordinal, interval, etc,. Deciding on the type of data to collect may, in the long term, save you time. You only collect what you need. Use your pilot study to sort out any issues around data collection. The population from which you collect the sample and the sample size can also influence the type of test to use.

Population and probability

Populations

Two important concepts associated with inferential statistics are those of population and probability. Mention has already been made of populations with respect to the selection of samples. Statisticians use the word 'population' in a different sense. With inferential statistics, if a particular test indicates that two (or more) sets of data, when analyzed, are significantly different, it is concluded that the data has been taken from two different populations. If no significant difference exists, the data has been taken from the same population. Statisticians apply the terms parametric and non-parametric with respect to populations. In a parametric population, the distribution of the characteristic being investigated follows a particular distribution. Statisticians have identified a number of different types of population distribution, for example, **normal**, **binomial** and **Poisson**. An example of a normal distribution is adult height. Most people hover around an average height with a small number of people being very tall or short. Binomial distribution is a frequency distribution where only two mutually exclusive outcomes are possible such as success or failure, loss or gain, and heads or tails if you were tossing a coin. Binomial statistics are used, for example, in clinical trials and opinion surveys where individuals have to choose between two possible products. The Poisson distribution is named after the French mathematician S.D. Poisson (1781–1840) who developed the concept. It occurs where a number of rare occurrences happen in a long series of trials. The number of stoppages in a food production line, and the number of accidents at a busy road junction, are examples of the Poisson distribution. With the two examples only the stoppages and accidents are studied, and not every product coming off the line and every car that uses the junction.

A non-parametric population is where no assumption is made about the distribution of the characteristic in question. Again, the choice of statistical test which can be applied will depend on whether you are dealing with a parametric or non-parametric population.

Probability

The words 'significantly different' have been used a number of times in connection with inferential statistics. It is essential to realize that statistical tests do not prove or disprove anything. They simply give a measure of the probability of a particular situation arising by chance alone or because of some other cause.

The probability of the sun not rising tomorrow is zero, or in percentage terms 0 per cent. Conversely, the probability that it will rise tomorrow is certain, or in percentage terms 100 per cent. It is possible, therefore, to give a numerical value, usually as a percentage, to different levels of probability and statisticians have worked out theoretical probability tables for all the commonly used statistical tests. In general terms, business works to a probability (p) of 5 per cent, or 0.05 as a decimal or 5:100 as a ratio. This is referred to as the 5 per cent significance level. It means that in 95 cases out of 100 any observed differences are due to the real differences existing, but in 5 cases out of 100 they will have arisen by chance alone.

Tests of significance can also be used in respect of correlation, as opposed to differences between two sets of data. Correlation is a technique which looks at the relationship between two independent variables. Probabilities have been calculated to show whether the relationship between two variables occurs by chance, or whether there is a real relationship, and as one variable changes so does the other.

Mean, median and mode

Certain numerical values appear a number of times in various statistical tests. They are the **mean**, **median** and **mode**. You may not need them all; it depends on the test used, but it is helpful to understand what they are. From a mathematical perspective they are all types of averages, each with particular advantages and limitations. The sources listed on pages 210–216 give more detail should you need it.

Mean

The mean is used in a number of tests and is sometimes referred to as the 'arithmetic mean'. For example, if five customers in our department store spent respectively £2, £6, £7, £10 and £5, the total spend would be £30. The average spend per customer or mean would be £6.

Median

The median is used in the sign test (see below). It is defined as the value of the middle item in a distribution. For example, imagine in our department store the number of purchases made by nine customers was follows:

7, 7, 2, 3, 4, 2, 7, 9 and 31

Arranged in order or rank they would be:

2, 2, 3, 4, 7, 7, 7, 9 and 31

The median value is ½ (9 + 1) i.e. the 5th value which is 7.

Mode

The mode is defined as the value that occurs most often. For example, suppose the store detective in the department store counted the number of stolen items in 25 shoplifters' bags and the results were as follows:

Number of stolen items in bags:	2	3	4	5	6
Frequency:	1	6	13	4	1

The mode number of stolen items is 4 which occurred 13 times, the next largest is 3 which had a frequency of 6.

Procedure for carrying out statistical tests of significance

All tests are carried out using the same basic scheme as follows.

STAGE 1

Two hypotheses are set up. Statisticians refer to these as the **null hypothesis** (referred to as H_0) and the **alternative hypothesis** (referred to as H_1). The null hypothesis states that for the test being carried out, nothing special has occurred and no real changes have taken place, i.e. no significant difference is present. The alternative hypothesis is that something special has occurred and a change has taken place, i.e. there is a significant difference.

STAGE 2

The chosen significance test is carried out and the appropriate statistic is calculated. This value is then compared to the critical value in the selected probability table appropriate to the chosen test.

STAGE 3

The calculated value and the theoretical critical value are compared. If the calculated value is less than the table's critical value, the null hypothesis (H_0) is not rejected. It is accepted and any differences are not significant; they could have happened by chance alone. However, if the calculated value is equal to, or greater than that listed in the table, the null hypothesis (H_0) is rejected, and the alternative hypothesis is accepted. In other words, significant differences exist; they are not due to chance alone. In most tests a probability of 5 per cent or 0.05 is used, which means that in 95 cases out of 100, real differences exist.

Examples of statistical tests

All are given in outline only. The annotated bibliography (page 210) lists books which give more detail.

NON-PARAMETRIC TESTS

These are tests which make no assumptions about the distribution of data. The data does not belong to any particular distribution. The tests only work on either nominal or ordinal data. This is data that can be put into either an order or rank.

- *Sign test.* This uses **nominal data**, and pairs of scores from repeated measures. It compares the number of differences between two conditions which are in the same direction. The null hypothesis states that there is no difference with respect to the scores. The alternative hypothesis states that there is a difference. An example would be a panel of people asked to compare an 'original' washing powder with a 'new improved' version of the same powder. The panel is asked to state if they feel the improved is better than the original, recording an improvement as (+) and no improvement as (–).

- *Wilcoxon signed rank test.* This test was devised by F. Wilcoxon (1892–1965). Born in Ireland he was a chemist and statistician and developed the test in the mid 1940s. The test uses data on the ordinal scale, and pairs of scores from repeated measures. The same null and alternative hypothesis are used as with the sign test. It is more sophisticated than the sign test, in that the differences are measured and then placed in rank order. With the above washing powder example, the volunteers would be asked to grade the improvement on a numerical scale, e.g. 1 to 5, and the values could then be ranked.

- *Mann-Whitney U test.* An example would be a company with two separate factories, one having a greater absenteeism record than the other. Collected data needs to be ordinal. In the example, the number of absences on a daily basis for a given time from each factory could be collected. The results from both factories could then be ranked as if one group, with the lowest number of absences recorded as one, and the highest number of absences being the top number. The null hypothesis would expect no differences, that is the scores would be randomly distributed across the two factories. If, however, most of the low-ranked scores came from one factory, and most of the high-ranked scores came from the other factory, this would signify that real differences exist between the two factories.

- *The Chi-squared test.* This is a popular test, and used a lot in market research. There are a number of variations, all of which use nominal data. It must be noted that chi-square does not work on individual scores, but frequencies, i.e. the number of times one event occurs. The basis of chi-square is that it compares the observed result with the expected result. In most calculations the expected result is 50–50. For example, suppose you carry out a survey to investigate people's preference for instant or real coffee, your observed results may be 70 per cent of your sample prefer instant coffee and 30 per cent, real coffee. You would regard your expected result as 50 per cent like instant, and 50 per cent like real coffee. You would then compare the observed results, i.e. 70 per cent and 30 per cent with the expected, i.e. 50 per cent and 50 per cent, and determine whether there was a significant difference.

PARAMETRIC TESTS

Tests in this group assume that the population has a particular distribution – normal, Poisson or binomial. Only interval and ratio data can be used. With some tests the sample size needs to be fixed at the start.

- *The Student's* t *test*. This test is well known, and is used to compare means from small samples, each usually less than 30. The test was first described in 1908 by W.S. Gosset. He worked for the Guinness family, and because he was not allowed to use his own name he published the work under the name of Student. The null hypothesis states that there are no significant differences between the means. There are variations of the *t* test, depending whether you are using paired or unpaired samples.
- *The Analysis of Variance (ANOVA).* This is a more complicated statistical procedure, and a number of variations exist. It is used when you want to compare two or more sample means to measure significant differences.

Summary

This chapter has reviewed the main methods for interpreting the results of your research. Irrespective of whether you have used a qualitative or quantitative approach, remember that your judgement as an independent researcher is important. The results of your research, presented in the correct format, are the evidence to support your views and ideas.

The key points included in the chapter are:

- The way(s) to approach qualitative data analysis.
- The use of specialized software to help evaluate qualitative data.
- The role of grounded theory and qualitative research.
- The preparation of data for quantitative analysis and the factors influencing quantitative data analysis.
- The role of descriptive statistics and the use of figures, graphs and diagrams.
- The use of inferential statistics including the importance of populations, probability and the use of mean, median and mode.
- A general plan for carrying out a statistical test for the non-parametric and parametric distributions.

9   Writing up your dissertation

Introduction

Finally, there comes a point when all the material has to be collated and written up to produce the final dissertation. A dissertation that is well written and presented creates a good impression; this is essential for getting your ideas and arguments across to the examiner. On the other hand, poor academic writing with sloppy presentation distracts the reader, and this will count against you. In a well-supervised dissertation, the task of writing will be encouraged from the very beginning. As already noted a research diary nurtures a writing habit from the outset. This should work hand in hand with notes following supervisor meetings, literature review notes and any other longer pieces of writing. Together they will form the basis for the chapters reflecting developmental points of progression throughout the work on your dissertation.

In most universities, nevertheless, the final written dissertation forms a major proportion of a student's final assessment on both undergraduate and postgraduate programmes. At PhD level it is almost entirely the case that the written dissertation is the focus of examination. Chapter 10 looks more closely at the assessment of dissertations.

Many lecturers would argue that, irrespective of the subject, a dissertation is the best indicator of a student's true ability on any programme. In reality, the dissertation can be a very unfair method of assessment, since it is only the final product, the written up and bound dissertation, that is marked. The processes you have gone through, the problems you may have faced and how you solved them, if not included in some way in the final write up, may go unnoticed. Although in certain institutions the proposal and ongoing meetings with supervisors form part of the final mark, in many universities it is still only the final document that is assessed. The task of writing up and producing the final dissertation is, therefore, very important. It must reflect the considerable effort and care you put into it.

As far as possible, the writing up should be completed as you go along. Writing is very much part of the total research process and many sections like the literature review may already be in draft. You now need to pull all the sections together in order to produce the final copy. It is essential that the final version reads as one document; it should run smoothly from the first page to the last. It sometimes happens that a dissertation may be disjointed: it is written in a formulaic way as a number of separate sections, only linked by a common author and title. Even though the dissertation is divided into separate chapters or sections, at the final writing up stage you must give it coherence and a sense of continuity.

Organizing an approach to academic writing

The dissertation, as a piece of writing, examines a number of important skills including information retrieval, problem solving, academic criticism and communication. Crucially for doctoral work, and while perhaps to a lesser extent but nonetheless important for Masters and undergraduate dissertations, examiners will look for four key qualities in their examination of the writing. These reflect a search for evidence at the required level of academic scholarship achieved by the student and include:

1. *Critical thinking*. This is the rational analysis and interpretation of knowledge. It includes crucially the contextual re-ordering and synthesis of theory, ideas and related information on the selected topic of the dissertation. At doctoral level this is literally the 'thesis' or conceptual framework and argument underpinning a new contribution to knowledge. Bachelors and Masters should attempt to provide the same kind of original contribution, although to a lesser extent. To achieve this, your work should contain critical thinking that demonstrates independent thinking that makes new connections and/or points to differences between your own and other work in the field. Always avoid writing an uncritical or descriptive account of various sources in the literature in your own work.

2. *The research*. This is the organization of the subject knowledge content, data and its interpretation. It represents the substance of your study. It is your own original work. Writing this up is in essence a research report. Make it a clear account of your own understanding of the topic, building upon a stated **rationale** for your approach to the research topic. The presentation of the research content will usually be an explanation of the empirical method used for data management and the findings reached by the researcher. Very often, this is presented as a new way of applying previous research to a new problem, and/or proving a '**hypothesis**', prediction or yet a more detailed stated proposition. Make your dissertation a best-case example; a set of

sections or chapters that allow the examiner and other readers to see how the research has been conducted and reached its conclusion. An excellent dissertation will be read and the research followed up in the future by other researchers interested in advancing the same area of knowledge in the field.

3. *Academic integrity.* The researcher (you) engaged in writing a dissertation must show, and hopefully follow, a commitment to research ethics that includes: firstly, a careful observation of ethical protocols associated with the conduct of research; secondly, show that care has been taken in the design of the research to ensure its veracity and **validity**; and, thirdly, the use of referencing and citation to demonstrate a commitment to avoid **plagiarism** and respect intellectual ownership of knowledge in the academic field. This is usually associated with a particular kind of academic writing that avoids exaggeration or dramatic flourish.

4. *Academic style.* This represents the kind of writing most suitable for the task in hand. The writing style adopted should always use precise and readable prose. Avoid very descriptive and emotional language and be concerned to offer a clear and logical account of the research completed. It is a little trickier to successfully present an argument without some appeal to emotion. Always avoid trying to be complicated or elaborate. The writing should show that you are well-organized and present ideas in logical order, as well as set out a fair or impartial perspective when presenting your inter-pretation, findings or position on a topic. There are useful sets of academic writing conventions that can help develop an academic writing style including use of citation, referencing, format and structure. Further examples of key features in good academic writing are explained later in this chapter.

Always try to think of the audience for your writing, and what is the purpose of the writing. The main 'audience' and 'target' for your work in writing a dissertation, are other researchers and, of course, the academics who will be your examiners.

The increasing availability of open online educational resources (OER) provides additional information on good practice in academic writing, and as well as a range of skills and strategies for the researching student. For example, visit http://www2.le.ac.uk/projects/oer/oers/ssds/student-support-and-development-service-oers at the University of Leicester. The OER dealing with the Harvard Referencing Manual and the OER on Writing Skills are worth taking a look at for useful advice. But as we previously suggested in Chapter 1, beware any tempta-tion to simply cut and paste material, or indeed purchase off-the-shelf writing from the Internet.

Practicalities: what is the best approach to writing up your dissertation?

Plan a realistic time schedule for writing up, and then stick to it. Remember that this should include time for writing, word processing, printing and binding your work. It is all too easy to fall behind schedule, and very difficult to catch up again.

Start writing up as soon as you have gathered any material, don't keep putting it off, or you will end up with huge amounts of data that are very difficult to sort out. If one aspect of the work is going slowly, don't be afraid to leave it for a few days, and return to it another time. Don't, however, use it as an excuse and stop work altogether; get on with writing up a different section. The change of material helps you see the overall context. Because dissertations are so long, you can often lose sight of this and can get bogged down in one section, especially if that section appears to be difficult to write.

With any of this 'formative writing' even though you are in the writing up stage, don't think of it as the final draft, just get your ideas down on paper. You can modify and improve it later. Don't spend hours perfecting one sentence – in the long run it is more effective to correct and change a first, but incomplete draft.

Always try to avoid one of the greatest pitfalls for the student wrestling with a closing deadline. Keep a note of any references you use, so that when you come to write your references and **bibliography** it will not be such a huge job. Academic referencing always seems to cause lots of problems, but in reality it can be straightforward, and full details on how to compile references are given at the end of this chapter.

If you do these things as you go along, by the time you are ready to refine the final draft, you will be able to concentrate on revising your existing writing into an acceptable style, rather than having to start from scratch. There is also an added advantage that you can directly ask your supervisor to helpfully comment on the style and clarity in your writing.

How to start writing up

A familiar stage in any stage of academic writing is to experience the 'blank sheet whiteout'. The blank sheet of paper or empty screen leaves you wondering just how to make a start. Where to begin? We suggest recounting the stages you have gone through in the 'research journey' and asking yourself some very basic questions to help clarify your thoughts at this stage. You may have several pieces of draft writing. You are almost certain to have notes and other writing for the critical review of literature. At this point, the task is one of marshalling this material and using it as the basis for the writing up. So this means:

- You have researched a particular topic that interested you. What attracted you to it in the first place and why was it your final choice? With hindsight, would you select it again?
- You have reviewed the literature. How did it inform your thinking and research design? Scan the research proposal. Have you achieved all your stated aims and objectives?
- What methodological approach did you take and why? Which particular data collection techniques and methods did you finally select? How have you analyzed and interpreted the data? Do your findings support or refute a particular argument or theory?
- Do you think your work has been balanced? Did you remain objective throughout? Does it fit in and compare with the research of others?
- What general and specific conclusions has your research indicated? How do these relate back to the original research topic? Do they shed light or otherwise on any wider issues which may be involved?
- Would you say your research should influence professional practice in a particular field of business and management?
- If you could go back right to the beginning equipped with the knowledge and experience you have gained, would you do it in exactly the same way or make changes?

Obviously, you are not going to be able to answer all of these questions, but going back to the start and thinking things through a second time can put them in perspective, and help you to see your dissertation as a whole.

Developing an appropriate academic writing style

Academic writing can be regarded as a very particular type of prose. It is associated with a traditional convention and the following distinguishing features. It is:

- *Somewhat specialized.* It is written for a specific audience and attempts to put forward a well-balanced view about the topic under investigation. It constantly refers to published work (with appropriate referencing), theory and results.
- *Produced in an 'academic style'.* That is, the passive voice and third person are most frequently used (e.g. 'a survey was carried out' *not* 'I carried out a survey') when describing research and conclusions, and always uses evidence to back up theories and ideas. Practise writing up your work in the same manner. Once you start to think about writing in an academic style, and

begin to use it, you will find it is easier to get your ideas across. It's worth mentioning here that certain areas (e.g. action research) now encourage writing in the first person – check with your supervisor what's best for you.

- **Well planned and thought through.** Time spent at the early planning stages is never wasted. It will make your written argument more coherent and focused. Careful planning helps in formulating a logical sequence and stops you missing out certain pieces of important information. The idea of systematic research, a rational argument and a rationale for your work is key to completing a successful dissertation.

- **Coherent and has a strong direction.** Have all your data well organized, and you will be able to concentrate on the structuring of your arguments at the writing up stage. As you write, think about the argument you are trying to put across, and the questions you need to answer. This will keep your writing focused. Each topic should connect to the last one, so that a coherent argument is developed. Don't think of each section as an essay in itself; each theme should flow from the preceding one, and in this way you will find that the dissertation becomes a whole rather than a collection of disconnected themes. Always try to present a balanced discussion linking one section of your writing with the next. Use the format of the dissertation to help here. Give each part a short introduction to explain 'the story so far and where it's going'.

- **Original, with no plagiarism or excessive paraphrase**. Always use your own words and never be tempted to copy out other people's writing. This is plagiarism. Plagiarism can be defined as taking and using someone else's writing, ideas or thoughts and passing them off as your own. When writing a dissertation you may come up against a difficult concept which you need to include, and at first glance it may seem a lot easier to copy out someone else's writing, or summarize, i.e. paraphrase their writing. The problem is that you will never understand the concept you are writing about. More importantly, if this is discovered when your dissertation is marked, the chances are you will fail your dissertation. Plagiarism and paraphrase are regarded as serious offences. Most universities now use an analytic software programme, such as Turnitin to screen all submitted work to identify plagiarism and will come down heavily on the guilty student. If you have some doubt about this aspect of academic writing at any point check it out with your supervisor. More generally, always ensure you acknowledge the source of ideas you pick up and use, whether in the development of your argument or discussion, or with direct use of citation.

  You should realize, nonetheless, that it is expected that you use people's ideas and quotations, provided that you acknowledge and/or cite them in your writing. Academic writing always contains references to other published works. It gives your work credibility, as it shows you are aware of the current literature in your field of study. Published work can also be used as evidence to support your line of argument. There are different conventions and ways of citing other people's writing. The most popular is known as the Harvard system and this is explained later in this chapter.

- *Well-presented, with correct spelling, grammar and punctuation.* Modern software packages and word processing facilities can help you make your dissertation look attractive and easy to read. A well-written document is better for being well produced and presented, and it is now possible to word process and print documents that were once in the realm of the professional printer. Good presentation, however, is not a substitute for good clear writing. Good writing involves using the correct grammar, spelling and punctuation. It is essential to get these correct if you want your writing to have academic credibility. Finally, don't go overboard with printer effects. You are not producing a brochure to recommend a particular software package. Check university regulations and ensure you apply the required font size and format (usually 12 point, double spaced, with specific margins), the print style, layout of headings, etc. and be consistent all the way through your document. Don't rely entirely on spelling and grammar checkers now available on many word processing packages. Although they can check the spelling of words like practise and practice, stationery and stationary, discreet and discrete, there and their, the words are checked in isolation and not in context. For example, which of the following sentences is correct – 'The manager in charge of stationary had a discrete conversation about bad practise in his factory' or 'The manager in charge of stationery had a discreet conversation about bad practice in his factory'?

Dissertation format

Most programmes provide guidelines on how to set out a dissertation. If these are not available to you, the following scheme is suggested. Even with guidelines, the advice should prove useful.

The overall objective is to produce a clear, easy-to-follow document. A dissertation is presented in a series of headed chapters or sections. It should be an original piece of work that argues convincing and persuasive conclusions drawn from a substantial body of collected data and material. The overall arrangement of a dissertation is best in three sections:

1. *Introductory chapters*
   These set out the relevant contextual and theoretical background information, and the reasons for studying the topic. They give an overview of the methodological approach and the data collection techniques used.

2. *Central and middle chapters*

   This is the main body of your dissertation. It is the location of 'the research' as previously explained. The exact number of sections or chapters will depend on the nature of your topic, but you would normally include the literature review, methodology and results. If you are adopting a **case study** approach involving a particular company or organization, you will need a section describing and explaining the case example. With action research these middle sections could be in the form of a story or narrative providing an account of research enquiry.

3. *The concluding chapters*

   The final chapters, usually termed conclusion and discussion, pull the whole work together. They relate your research findings to the initial aims and objectives set out at the start. These concluding sections must present an overview of the preceding chapters without simply repeating earlier material. They should be used to reflect on the whole process of the dissertation, and attempt to explain where the research could lead if it was to be continued.

In addition to the above, the dissertation should contain an **abstract**, contents page, acknowledgements and a bibliography. A suggested, more detailed format is now given, in the order in which these features should appear, followed by specific advice for each section. Certain sections are sometimes known by alternative names and these are given in brackets.

Suggested format

Title page
Acknowledgements
Abstract
Contents page
Introduction (background to study)
Literature review
Methodology and data collection
Results (observations, findings)
Discussion
Conclusions (sometimes includes recommendations)
Bibliography (references cited)
Appendices

Depending on your dissertation, you may need a glossary of terms and abbreviations and a signed declaration that the work is your own. Some institutions require students to provide separate lists of tables and figures in addition to the contents page.

Title page

Here you include the title of the dissertation, your full name and, depending on your university, you may need to include details of your degree, enrolment number, and university department.

Acknowledgements

It is always a good idea to thank everyone who has helped you with your work. No-one likes being taken for granted. It is common practice to thank your supervisor and other members of the academic staff who may have provided extra support with particular sections. If you have worked in a company during the dissertation, don't forget to thank them as well. Always check the spellings of names, initials and qualifications of the people you include.

Abstract

The abstract should be a summary of the whole work. It should be brief, no more than a few hundred words, and to the point. It should contain no examples or other substantiating information, but simply be an outline of the work. An abstract should be complete in its own right. It is often easier to write the abstract when all the work is finished. Do not include references in an abstract.

Contents page

All dissertations need a well laid out contents page. Usually chapters and sections are numbered using Arabic numbers (1, 2, 3, etc.) and appendices in Roman numerals (I, II, etc.). The contents page is one of the first things the reader sees, but one of the last that is completed. It is important that it is accurate, so always double-check to ensure, for example, that Chapter 6 does really begin on page 45 and not 54. Errors like this creep in very easily towards the end of a piece of writing when you are tired and want to get it finished, but they do mar the overall impression of the work. With respect to numbering, page 1 normally starts at the introduction. The title page, acknowledgements, abstract, contents page are normally numbered i, ii, iii, etc.

Introduction

This should state clearly and concisely what it is you are setting out to achieve. The aim and plan of the dissertation should be made explicit here; do not spring any surprises on your reader later on. Tell the reader why you chose your topic, what the main research issues are, what aspects you investigated and how you investigated them.

Literature review

With every dissertation a review of previously published work is included. The review shows how your work relates to what other researchers have done. It sets your dissertation in the context of existing knowledge. Re-read the last two sentences and note the word 'relates' and the phrase 'context of existing knowledge'. With the literature review it is essential that you show quite clearly how your investigation compares and links with what has been done before. A review is not a catalogue of references arranged in chronological order, each one briefly summarized. Rather, your writing should pick out trends and patterns, giving and explaining reasons for and against a particular situation. It must relate theory to practice and argue why in certain situations established theories and ideas may or may not be accepted. In summary, it should provide a critical insight into the topic under investigation. It is a critical and analytic review of ideas, theories and argument that forms a basis for bringing your own perspective to the topic.

Methodology and data collection

In this section you describe and explain how you studied the topic of your investigation. Include a full account of your choice of techniques and why you adopted a **mixed**, **qualitative** or **quantitative methodology**. Each single method of data collection needs to be described, together with full information on any sampling technique you employed. Details of any pilots used should be included and how they may have influenced your final data collection. If triangulation was used, this also needs to be written up. Don't forget to include in this section the techniques used to interpret the collected data. The methodology section should be detailed enough for another researcher to repeat your work. The results they collect and their interpretation may be different, but this is another story. This section is often very straightforward and is a good place to begin writing the dissertation. You are writing up an account.

Results

Results can range from transcriptions of **interviews** to tables of raw data. This section only describes the results obtained. Refrain from explaining what they mean. This comes in the next section. It is very easy to comment on the results when describing them, but this can be confusing for the reader. In this section you would include a full analysis of how you interpreted the data and give details of any calculations. If you have collected data in a number of different ways, keep each one separate. In this section you can include tables and figures to summarize your quantitative results, and describe the trends and concepts identified from qualitative analysis. With certain quantitative investigations you may have collected vast amounts of data. In these situations summarize the data with the use of tables and only include the summaries in the main dissertation. The original data can either be included in an appendix or can be submitted as a separate file. It might be a good idea to discuss this with your dissertation supervisor.

Discussion (interpretation of the results)

In this section you answer a number of questions. You interpret what your research findings mean and whether they agree with the aims and objectives set out in your proposal. You relate your work back to the literature review and see how it fits in with all the published work. How does it compare with established theories and ideas? Are there similarities and differences and why? If you have taken a grounded theory approach, how has the theory developed? Are there any generalizations you can make? You also need to include in the discussion an account of the appropriateness of your methodology and data collection techniques, and whether in hindsight they were the most suitable. The discussion is a very important section of the dissertation, and should also demonstrate how your research relates to the wider context of the subject. It is not an easy section to write, and is often best started by using a series of topic headings as a guide. These include:

- the relationship of the results to the objectives set out in the proposal;
- the relationship to published literature;
- the role of theory, grounded or otherwise;
- the appropriateness of the methodology and data collection;
- the effect on professional practice.

It is very easy when writing the discussion to include general points that, although important, do not arise from your work. You must base your writing in this section on the work you have done. Although you can use evidence from the literature, it must support your views and opinions. We recommend you do this sparingly, if at all, in this section.

Conclusion

This is the final section, and because it is the last one it is important to write it as well as you can. Include the following elements:

- a summary of the principal features of your study;
- an outline of the main findings, key concepts and theories identified in the literature;
- the implications involved by reflecting on your study as a practitioner and a researcher;

- any recommendations for future research and practical suggestions which may influence the practice of business and management.

The conclusion finally must not simply become a summary of your own and other people's work. The two must integrate in a further consideration of your own claim to making a contribution to the discipline (academic and/or theoretical significance), to the field or applied context (professional or social impact), and lastly but perhaps most importantly, to the author (personal learning and professional practice). An excellent and safe dissertation will include a compelling case for securing all three forms of implications or impact of the research.

Bibliography

The bibliography should be presented according to a recognized academic format. The **Harvard system** described later is popular and recommended. Certain universities ask students to distinguish between references actually cited in the text and general works not cited which may have informed their thinking.

Appendices

If you have any material that you produced or gathered during the dissertation process that you feel is relevant, but would break up the flow of your argument if placed in the main text, then consider including it as an appendix. Any letters/ replies, large amounts of data, copies of questionnaires and interview schedules, etc. that are too detailed to place in the main body of the work, can be included as appendices. Do, however, be sparing in your use of appendices, and don't include material simply to pad the work out. Only include essential information. Usually appendices are not included in the word length of a dissertation. Always ensure any material placed in the appendices is referred to within the text. Otherwise, the material should not be included.

Keep to the regulations

All universities have regulations with respect to the submission of dissertations. Don't assume that you will be allowed to deviate from these – you won't. The authors knew a student who was not initially granted his degree because his dissertation was bound in the wrong colour! He presented his work in black and the university regulations stipulated blue. He had to have his work rebound before he could graduate. Check on the following:

- *Submission date.* Does your dissertation have to be handed in by a certain date? Obtain a receipt when you hand it in.
- *Length.* What is the minimum and maximum word length? Does this include appendices, bibliography etc?

- *Declaration*. Most universities require the student to produce a signed and dated declaration that the work is all their own, and has not been previously submitted for another degree. All reference to other people's work must be acknowledged. Universities regard plagiarism as a very serious offence and, if proven, it will certainly stop you getting your degree.
- *Page layout.* Do you have to conform to any special page layout with respect to margin size, font, point size, single or double spacing, position of headers and footers, page numbering, etc.? All of these seem very minor points, but together are important to the overall presentation of your work.
- *Number of copies.* How many copies of the final work do you have to hand in?
- *Overall layout and structure.* Do check: are you expected to follow a prescribed layout and arrange the various chapters in a particular order?
- *Binding.* Some universities expect dissertations, especially at postgraduate level, to be professionally bound like a book. Some allow spiral binding, and some let students hand in their work in a loose-leaf A4 ring folder. Many universities now have their own bindery. This makes things easier as the bindery will be able to advise on the correct procedure. Note: having your work bound costs money – it's not cheap.
- *Referencing system.* All references must be cited in the text, together with a bibliography. Are you expected to use a particular referencing system?

Additional advice on writing up

The following are general points that may also help at the writing up stage:

- *Format.* The unfamiliar format of a dissertation often causes problems. Having to write an abstract, contents page, acknowledgements, etc. can present some students with difficulties simply because they have not had to do them before. Most of these things should be left until the main body of the work has been written, so don't worry about them at first. Get started on your research, and as you read about your topic, take a look at some dissertations in the library, you will gradually become more familiar with their format.
- *Word count.* Be aware of the required length of the dissertation, and estimate how many words you are going to include in each section. This way you can check as you go along whether your work is going to meet the required length at the end. Students who are used to writing shorter essays and reports are unfamiliar with producing a piece of work that may be about 25 000 words. In consequence they often produce a number of standard-length essays of about 2 000 words and try to fit them together to the required word count. This doesn't work, as the final dissertation does not

hang together as one coherent piece of well-argued writing. You must ensure that each chapter follows on logically from the last, and that the whole work follows a line of argument from introduction to conclusion. A similar concern for establishing the golden thread of continuity is especially relevant to a doctoral dissertation, which usually involves a word count of more than 60 000 and sometimes up to 100 000 words. A number of students become worried when they have too many words. This is a good position to be in; far better than to have too few words. It means you have a lot of information. A number of devices can sometimes help cut down the word number. For example, remove words like also, very, usually, and often. This can save in total around 200 words. Flow charts and diagrams can take the place of long descriptions. Finally, use appendices effectively.

- *Using tables and figures*. If your work would be clearer and easier to understand through the use of tables or diagrams (always called figures), etc. then include them. If you are putting one in to fill out a chapter, then don't include it. Make sure tables and figures are easy to understand, and help to explain your work. If they are irrelevant or superfluous they may confuse the reader and detract from your work. Also, they need to be referenced if taken from another source.
- *Being too descriptive.* The most common complaint about dissertations is that the writing is too descriptive. To avoid this error make sure you set out to prove something, and present evidence to back up your assertions. You should not simply describe something, but rather analyze it by saying why it is the way it is, and how it could be improved. A dissertation should always include at its heart an 'argument'. Note the word 'thesis', an alternative to dissertation, is literally a 'propositional argument' as defined in the dictionary.
- *Using evidence.* Always use evidence to back up any assertions you make, and make it clear how you arrived at your conclusions. State clearly whether the evidence you use is your own, or if you are basing your conclusions on the work of others. If the latter is the case, make sure you include references to your sources. As mentioned before, avoid plagiarism at all times – if in doubt put in the appropriate reference; it is better to include too many than too few.

Advice on references, footnotes, quotations and other points of style

Quoting references

There are different ways of doing this and one of the most popular and universal methods in current use is the *Harvard system*. Here the author's surname and date of publication are used to identify a reference. In the text a reference would be cited as, 'some interesting results were obtained (White, 1985)'. If the author's surname is part of the sentence, then the date alone is sufficient, for example, 'White (1985) reported some interesting results'. It is customary to use parentheses as shown. If reference to a specific page or diagram is required, as opposed to the whole work, then the following technique applies, 'analysis of the results (White, 1985, p. 13, Table 2)', or 'White (1985, p. 13, Table 2) in his results indicated ...'.

At the end of the text the information sources are listed alphabetically by surnames. If the same author has published several works in one year they are identified as 1952a, 1952b, 1952c, and so on, both in the written text and in the reference list at the end of the writing. An advantage with this method is that references can be either easily added or removed.

Constructing the bibliography or 'references'

The preparation of the bibliography always seems to present students with unnecessary difficulty. They are often uncertain as to how much detail for each reference should be included. Examples of different types of information sources are now given showing what details should be recorded, and how each could be set out in a list using the Harvard system. It is an accepted convention that certain words are underlined (if typed or hand-written) or italicized (if word processed or printed). Some authors and publishers recommend slightly different ways of setting out from that given below: for example, the use of capital letters for authors' names, enclosing dates of publication in parentheses, reversing the order of publisher and place of publication, and minor changes in punctuation. The important point is to adopt a system that provides enough detail so that the reader of your work could locate a copy of the same reference without undue difficulty. All of this can seem complicated. There will be specific guidance at your university on the recommended citation convention to use and study guides are usually available to provide further support. An example of this can be found at http://www.learntech.uwe.ac.uk/referencing/Default.aspx?pageid=1803.

EXAMPLES OF DETAILS TO RECORD

The following detail is what you should seek to record as you read and compile notes to assist in writing up at a later point in the literature review process

1. Textbook

Record: Author surname(s) and initial(s), date of publication, title of book, edition (except the first), place of publication and publisher. Include page numbers, tables and figures if reference has been made to specific parts of the book.

> Stannack, P. (1993) *Managing People for the First Time: Gaining Commitment and Improving Performance*. London: Pitman.

2. A paper in a periodical

Record: Author surname(s) and initial(s), date of publication, title of article, name of journal, volume (and part number if applicable), inclusive pages of paper.

> Harrigan, K. R. (1985) An Application of Clustering for Strategic Group Analysis. *Strategic Management Journal,* Vol. 6, pp. 55–73.

Some journals have long titles and some form of abbreviation is acceptable. However, never make up your own, since if everyone did this, it would soon cause chaos and confusion. To be on the safe side never use abbreviations and give journal titles in full.

3. An edited book with every chapter written by a different author

Many books have each chapter written by a different author, and the whole book is edited by someone else. In these instances record, for the chapters used, author surname(s) and initial(s), date of publication, title of chapter, page number(s), editor'(s') surname(s) and initial(s), title of book, place of publication, publisher.

> Eisenhardt, K. M. (1995) Building Theories from Case Study
> Research, pp. 65–90 in Huber, G. P. and Van de Ven, A. H. (eds)
> *Longitudinal Field Research Methods: Studying Processes of
> Organizational Change.* London: Sage.

4. A thesis (or dissertation)

Record: Author surname(s) and initial(s), date, title of thesis, degree awarded, academic institution awarding the degree.

> Ritson, M. B. (1996) The Interpretation of Advertising Meaning. PhD thesis.
> University of Lancaster.

5. A report

Various types of reports are available, but they can be extremely difficult to trace, since many writers give too little information in their reference lists. Always provide enough detail. If the report has been the responsibility of a particular person (normally the chair-person of the committee writing the report) then classify the report according to their surname.

> Taylor, F. J. W. (1994) *Management Development to the Millennium.
> The Taylor Working Party Report. The Way Ahead 1994–2001.* Corby:
> The Institute of Management.

If the report has been prepared for an official organization, and the authorship is uncertain, then use the name of the organization in quoting and listing the reference. For example,

Advisory Board for the Research Councils (1983) *Scientific Opportunities and the Research Budget: A Report to the Secretary for Education and Science*. London: Department of Education and Science.

6. Unsigned articles in books, journals, newspapers, etc.

Often articles appear and the author's name cannot be traced. Refer to such articles, both in the text and the reference list, as anonymous together with their date. The word 'anonymous' may be abbreviated to 'anon'.

Anon (1994) The Iron is Cold. *The Economist*. Vol. 30, No. 7848 (29 January), p. 46.

7. Other books (e.g. data books, directories)

With certain types of reference book it is difficult to find the name of either the editor or author. In such cases give as much detail as possible.

8. Unpublished information

Although the majority of references will be from published material, occasionally you may learn of some interesting work possibly in a letter from, or during a conversation with, someone. It is acceptable to use this information, provided the person in question has no objection, and you keep this type of reference source to a minimum. Written work relying completely on information from unpublished work would lack credibility. Refer to this type of information source as a personal communication. In the text it would be acknowledged as, 'the results of the survey were not significant' (personal communication, 1987)'.

In the reference list the reference should be filed alphabetically under 'P', together with a short description as to the type of communication, for example, 'a letter' or 'conversation'. Many professional publishers instruct their authors to cite this type of source only in the text, and not include it in the reference list. For student work, however, it is good practice to include it as it shows to either a reader or examiner that you have consulted a wide variety of different sources.

9. Non-book sources

With this type of information source give as many details as possible. For example, with audio-visual material record the title, distribution or production company, date of production or release, production personnel, namely director and producer, and type of material (e.g. film, video, tape, slides). In practice, all this information may not be available, so record as much as you can.

10. Citing electronic sources

No official method has been adopted yet, and the following examples are guidelines only:

> *Email correspondence:* Sender, sender's email address, subject, date.
> *Electronic journal:* Author, date, title of article, journal title, volume, location, URL.
> *Internet site:* Author/editor, date, title, location of server, publisher/maintainer of site, URL.

As with citing traditional sources, it is important to be as consistent as possible. The technology is advancing all the time. When quoting electronic sources, try to include as much information as possible so the reader could locate the same source.

Footnotes

In academic writing footnotes are sometimes used to explain an unusual phrase or unfamiliar term, or to add extra information that would be awkward to include in the text. Footnotes are either asterisked or numbered. The numbering is either consecutive throughout the text, or at the start of each page or chapter. Try to keep footnotes down to a minimum. Footnote numbers can cause confusion and if the work is being typed or word-processed, the spacing of the footnotes at the bottom of the page can be difficult. Humanities students make great use of footnotes and sometimes use them to quote all their references, which reflect a different set of protocols for referencing.

Use of et al.

Articles and books are sometimes written by more than one author. If there are more than three authors (e.g. Machon, Walker, Holmes, and Nyland) the *et al.* (= *et alia,* Latin 'and others') can be used instead of quoting all four names. The reference would be referred to by the first author's name followed by *et al.,* for instance, Machon *et al.* The reference is quoted in this form in the text, but in full in the bibliography. The *et al.* is always underlined or printed in italics, and is always followed by a full stop.

Use of quotations

It is perfectly acceptable to use quotations to illustrate a particular point in your writing. Always keep each quotation to a minimum and normally no longer than two or three lines. Quotations of a paragraph or longer are best left out unless there is a particular reason to include them. Always quote correctly, and acknowledge either the source or reference. It improves the presentation if each quotation is indented slightly, and separated from the rest of the writing. Use single quotation marks at the beginning and end of each quotation. Students often fail to realize they can amend quotations to make them more relevant to the writing at hand. For instance, use square brackets if you wish to add something not present in the original quotation, but which would make its meaning clearer. For example,

'They [the unions] gave their approval to the decision'.

If the original author has made a mistake then use *sic* (Latin, meaning 'so written') to show there was an error in the original and you have not misquoted:

'The paper (*sic*) were put into the file'.

Here *sic* means that 'papers' should be read instead of 'paper'. Note *sic* is always underlined or italicized.

If you want to shorten a quotation, but wish to include some of it, then use … (three dots). For example:

'The cat … on the mat'.

Use of op. cit. *and* ibid.

Op. cit. and *ibid.* tend to be used mainly by humanities students either in footnotes or reference lists.

When used, both *op. cit.* and *ibid.* are always underlined or italicized. *Op. cit.* (= *opere citato,* Latin meaning 'in the work cited') is used when you are referring to a reference which has been mentioned earlier in the text, for instance, White, *op. cit.*, p.132. *Ibid.* (= *ibidem,* Latin meaning 'in the same place') is used in a footnote or a reference list if consecutive references have the same source even though the page numbers, etc. may be different.

Some final tips

- Enjoy the writing process. Although it is hard work, it is rewarding, and a well-written, neatly presented document gives a great feeling of satisfaction.
- Write up drafts as you go along throughout your research – don't leave it all to the end!
- Check your writing out with friends, colleagues and, of course, your supervisor.
- Leave yourself enough time to ensure any graphs, charts etc. can be well produced.
- Edit and re-edit to ensure you are using accessible language – avoid the idea that academic writing is theoretically complex or full of jargon as to be incomprehensible.

- Always check that your argument is logically sound and follows a line of progression through the dissertation. This is often referred to as the 'golden thread' pinning together the many separate stages of the research and parts of the writing to ensure the whole piece is greater than the sum of its parts. A poor dissertation is one with holes in its argument, gaps in its structure and an uneven or even fractured development.
- Proofread! Finally, scan for small errors and typographical mistakes. We all make these errors as word processing is now how a piece of writing is usually completed.
- One more thought: enjoy the moment when you can flick through the pages of the bound manuscript and remind yourself – this is all your own work.

Summary

This chapter has focused on finally writing up your dissertation and explains the stages involved.

The key points included in this chapter are:

- The key features of academic writing.
- The best way to approach and start the writing up process.
- How to develop an academic writing style.
- The correct format and layout of a dissertation, including the main features of each section.
- Advice about adhering to university regulations.
- The construction of a bibliography, and the citation of other people's work, together with other points of style.

10   The assessment of dissertations, including *vivas* and presentations

Introduction

This chapter is about how dissertations are marked and assessed. Depending on your course and university you may have a ***viva voce*** (oral examination) and give a presentation about your dissertation. These are also discussed in this chapter.

The assessment of dissertations

Students often ask how dissertations are marked and graded. A brief account of how this takes place and the standard expected may help you in the final stages of producing a dissertation. Mention has already been made that in some ways the whole process of assessing a dissertation is unfair. In some universities it is only the final product, the completed piece of work you submit, that is marked. This can be termed '**summative assessment**'. It means that the overall grade the student achieves on a degree programme is dependent entirely on the final pieces of work completed (e.g. final examinations, end assessments and dissertation, etc). The amount of time spent working on the dissertation is not reflected in the final mark. In some universities, however, the processes leading up to the completed work are taken into account. The proposal stage is graded together with a record of meetings with your supervisors. This is termed '**formative assessment**'. Formative assessment attempts to take into account the student's overall learning experience when arriving at the final grade.

Procedures of marking

The mechanics of marking vary depending whether you are enrolled on either an undergraduate or postgraduate course. All universities publish assessment regulations for all their courses. Moreover, with respect to the dissertation you may have to hand in more than one copy, especially if you are on a Doctorate programme. Check out your regulations.

Undergraduate programmes

On a Bachelor's degree a dissertation is marked usually by two members of staff. The first marker is normally your supervisor and the second marker is another lecturer who has expertise in the overall subject area of your dissertation. Each marker marks independently, and then they meet to agree the final mark. If they cannot agree the mark then a third member of staff is called in to resolve the problem.

There is also the system of external examiners. A selection of dissertations is sent to the external examiner who vets the overall standard of marking to ensure parity between students. An external examiner is normally a lecturer from another university who has a great deal of experience in examining at a particular level. In most UK institutions undergraduate dissertations scoring over 70 per cent are graded first class, 60–69 per cent are graded upper second class, 50–59 per cent are graded lower second class and 40–49 per cent are graded third class. Dissertations scoring below 40 per cent are either recorded as a fail or a pass, depending on different university regulations.

Postgraduate programmes

Masters degrees

The marking on a Masters course is similar to that on undergraduate programmes. The work is marked by two staff members, and a third is called in if needed. There is also the external examiner who looks at a number of dissertations. Masters degrees tend to be graded differently from Bachelors degrees. Some universities keep the first, second and third class system; others grade by awarding a distinction, merit or pass. Check with your university's regulations as to which scheme operates. In most UK universities if the total mark is 70 per cent or above, the dissertation is classed at distinction level. In the UK a percentage system of marking is used, but in other European and overseas countries different systems can operate, such as a letter system (A – F where A is good and F is poor) or a number system (1 – 10 where 10 is good and 1 is poor). With some Masters courses, *viva* examinations and/or presentations are part of the assessment.

Doctorate degrees

The assessment of doctoral work is different in that it tends to be more formal and always involves a *viva* examination. A panel of about three or more staff question the student about their work. On the panel is the external examiner(s), an internal examiner (not always the supervisor), the supervisor (if not examining) and a senior staff member of the university usually acts as chair. The range of questions asked at the *viva* is considered below. Most universities have Research and Higher Degrees Committees which arrange and oversee the examination of PhD and Professional Doctorates. If you are on a doctoral programme read and thoroughly understand the regulations relevant to your degree. Doctorates are not normally graded – they either pass or fail. Often at the end of a *viva* the degree is awarded subject to changes in the dissertation. For example, more discussion regarding the methodology or greater evaluation of the research results may be needed. Also, with some Doctorate degrees a presentation is also required.

What examiners look for when they mark

Irrespective of the degree and level, nowadays most dissertations are marked against what are termed '**assessment criteria**'. Criteria act in a way like standards against which your work is judged. Assessment criteria provide a framework for the marking of dissertations. This helps to ensure parity between students. Exact details of the criteria will vary from institution to institution, but the following general statements may help you gauge the standard of your work.

Remember each university has its own way of assessment. This can vary from department to department, and degree to degree. Some universities use a standardized marking scheme and an allocation of marks is given for individual criteria. Others are less formal and award an overall mark. Also with postgraduate courses the student is expected to satisfy and achieve the criteria to a greater extent than at undergraduate level.

Compare your work against the criteria. Does the final dissertation satisfy the criteria listed? Some of the criteria may appear over-prescribed, for example, is the pagination correct and accurate? However, the final dissertation must be as polished and professional as you can make it. The dissertation you submit is the evidence on which the work is graded. What appear as minor errors to you may give the examiners the overall impression that the work has been rushed and quickly put together. Don't give marks away. Untidy presentation, bad grammar, and misspellings lose marks. They may make the difference between either pass or fail.

The assessment criteria are grouped under a range of headings. The list below is not exhaustive, but should cover most of the points looked for in the assessment of dissertations.

1. **Introduction, aims and overall approach**

    Is the dissertation thoroughly related to a chosen area of business and management, and the named award?

Does the title suggest a clear business and management theme?
Has the scope of the dissertation been accurately defined?
Is there a well-argued academic **rationale** for the work?
Is there a well-presented and lucid account of the aims?
Is there evidence that there is a depth of understanding of the subject area?
Is an overview of the work given and explained?

2. **Use of the literature**

Has the student made extensive use of the literature?
Has a wide range of different primary and secondary sources been accessed?
Are the sources used up-to-date and appropriate to the dissertation?
Is the information retrieval complete in depth and breadth?
Is there emphasis in the use of research-based literature?
Have all sources been cited in an appropriate **academic style**?
Does the student show a thorough understanding of the key theories and
  concepts involved?
Has there been an appropriate selection of theoretical material?
Has the literature been reviewed in an academic sense in that relevant themes
  and ideas have been identified and compared?
Is there evidence that the literature has informed the overall thinking behind the
  dissertation and the methodological approach adopted?

3. **Methodological issues and data collection**

Is there awareness that the selected research process is relevant to the
  dissertation?
Has the overall methodological approach been clearly explained?
Is there a well-reasoned rationale for the chosen approach?
Are the methods of data collection well-described and justified?
Are the limitations and benefits of the selected techniques identified and
  discussed?
Is there evidence that any chosen methods have been piloted?
Are the methods of analysis and interpretation described and explained?
Is there a clear understanding of the theoretical basis on which the data
  analysis has been carried out?

4. **Results, their analysis and interpretation**

Are the research findings clearly explained, easy to understand and
  well-presented?
Are the methods of analysis appropriate to the ways of data collection?
Have the findings been subjected to appropriate analysis?
Have the techniques and methods of analysis been systematically and
  thoroughly applied?

Have the limitations of the data analysis been considered?

Are the chosen methods of analysis suitable for the methodological approach and data collection methods used in the dissertation?

5. **Discussion and conclusion**

Have the research aims set out in the introduction been addressed?

Is the material presented in these sections well organized?

Have the conclusions been logically derived and supported by evidence presented in the earlier sections of the dissertation?

Has the relationship of theory to professional practice been discussed?

Does the research agree with, or challenge, accepted theory?

Does the student present a coherent argument with respect to results, theory and practice?

Is there an awareness of the limitations of the research?

Have the research findings been discussed in the context of other published work in terms of breadth, methodology and use of the literature?

Is there evidence of self-reflection?

Have future ideas based on the dissertation been identified and commented upon?

To what extent does the dissertation demonstrate originality and contribution to knowledge?

6. **Quality of presentation**

Is the dissertation presented in an accepted format (e.g. title page, abstract, introduction, aims, methodology, etc.)?

Is the text free from errors of spelling, punctuation and grammar?

Is the work correctly referenced using an accepted academic system?

Is the overall style and vocabulary mature, and appropriate to the subject and content of the dissertation?

Is the quality of tables, figures and other illustrations up to a professional standard?

Has the manuscript been accurately proofread?

Is the pagination correct and accurate?

Has there been effective use of quotations, cross-referencing, appendices and similar devices?

7. **General criteria**

In addition to the above there are also a number of general criteria which need to be taken into account. These include:

Has the dissertation adhered to the university's published guidelines with respect to ethical codes of practice?

Does the dissertation evidence good overall planning and organization?

Does the dissertation evidence the student's ability to work independently at an advanced level?

Has the scope of the dissertation been too broad or too narrow?

Is there a clear theme running through the entire dissertation?

Is there, all the way through, a coherent and clear academic argument that has been logically developed?

Is the overall level of analysis discursive rather than descriptive? Has the student related the research to wider, more general, areas of business and management?

Obviously, depending on your university, not every criterion will apply. Check what is required for your dissertation. Read carefully any published guidelines and regulations.

Viva voce examinations

At Masters and Doctorate level an oral examination or *viva voce* is common practice. At a *viva* you will be asked a series of questions about your dissertation. In the main the questions will reflect the assessment criteria listed above. The *viva* is normally conducted by one or more examiners, who may, or may not, include your supervisor. Occasionally the external examiner will be present. At Doctorate level the *viva* is more formal along the lines mentioned above. The length of a *viva* can vary from one to three hours, and normally you can take a copy of your dissertation in with you. The aim of an oral examination is to discover how well you know your work. Although you may be apprehensive at the prospect of an oral examination, regard it as an opportunity to demonstrate how good you are. You know your dissertation better than anyone. You, therefore, have the advantage! The type of questions will vary and the following list will give you a good idea what to expect. Note that a number of questions probe similar areas; the difference lies in the emphasis and focus. Also at postgraduate level your response to a question should reflect a real depth of understanding and knowledge. Be prepared to discuss your research at some length. The questions are designed to engage you in a meaningful academic debate about your work. You must be prepared to defend your dissertation, and demonstrate a thorough and rigorous understanding of the work.

Sample *viva* questions

- What is the academic contribution of your dissertation?
- How does your work build on existing areas of knowledge?

- How is your work original?
- What are the research objectives, and explain how you arrived at them?
- How does your work add to the body of knowledge of the subject as a whole?
- How does your research relate theory to practice?
- Has the research any commercial and practical application?
- How did the literature inform your thinking and approach to the work?
- How is the literature linked to the research objectives?
- How did the literature influence your choice of methodology?
- How do you justify your methodology and choice of data collection method(s)?
- Would you say that the focus of your work is subject-based, problem-based, or methodologically-based?
- During the research did you encounter any unexpected problems, and how did you overcome them?
- How is your research and methodology different from other researchers?
- How did the research objectives guide or influence the analysis of the data?
- How are the findings linked to the research objectives, literature, theory and practice?
- How did you arrive at your conclusions and why do you think they are valid?
- Are there any ethical issues identified in the dissertation?
- If you were to repeat the research, discuss, with reasons, if you would do it exactly the same way or make changes?
- With hindsight, do you have any suggestions as to where and how the research may be developed?
- Do you have any suggestions for further work?
- How do you think your research rates when compared against the work of established researchers in the field?
- How do your research results contribute to current thinking and debate about the subject?
- On reflection how would you assess the strengths and benefits, and weaknesses and limitations of your research?

Preparing for your *viva*

Often a *viva* is held sometime after you have submitted you dissertation. It is essential to remind yourself of its content. The following points may help you in preparing for the *viva*.

- Work through the dissertation and know what's in each chapter. Be able to answer questions on specific detail as well as on general themes and ideas.

It is perfectly acceptable to take into a *viva* notes about your dissertation. It is also a good idea to mark up with slips of paper particular pages which you think may come up in discussion.

- The questions might come in any order. You may be challenged about your conclusions and discussion before being asked about the aims, objectives and research methodology.
- When a question is asked jot down on a piece of paper the main points. If the question has a number of parts, answer by taking each part in turn. Be systematic and organized in the way you respond to questions. Don't rush an answer. Think before you speak. If a question is long and involved, and you are not exactly sure what is being asked, ask for clarification and for the question to be repeated, but don't interrupt before the question is complete.
- Before the *viva* try and find out about the staff who will be on the panel. What are their backgrounds and interests? It may help to give you confidence.
- Dress smartly, but don't go over the top. You must feel comfortable and relaxed, but appear business-like and professional.
- Expect to be nervous – once the questioning starts nerves seem to disappear.

Finally, although an oral examination can be quite rigorous, it is not a personal attack on you, it is the quality of your work that is being questioned. Remember it is a chance to demonstrate your expertise in a particular research area.

Presentations

Many universities now expect postgraduate students to give a presentation as part of their overall assessment for their dissertation. Some even record a selection of student presentations for moderation purposes. Again, this helps to ensure fairness and parity between students Presentations are very common in the world of business and most students have had plenty of experience. The prospect, however, of standing up and talking to a group of people, often strangers, can still cause stress. Hopefully the advice that follows will alleviate some of it. A number of universities now run workshops on presentation skills. Always attend and take part if these are available. With presentations, marks are awarded both for academic content and style of delivery. The assessment criteria noted above still apply with presentations. A certain percentage of the total mark for your dissertation may be awarded for the presentation. Check with your supervisor and the university regulations. With packages like PowerPoint, presentations can be very slick and professional. If you are nervous about presentations, look on them as a performance, which means you need to practise and rehearse beforehand.

The audience

Depending on your course the time allowed for a dissertation presentation will vary, but usually it is somewhere between 15–30 minutes with time at the end for questions. The audience will normally consist of an examiner (maybe your supervisor) and other staff members of the department. Remember, the audience is an essential part of your presentation. Your content, style and delivery are aimed at them. You should interest and inform, but never bore. The information you present is to be seen and heard and not read. Try to imagine yourself in the audience's place and think what it would be like to sit and listen to your presentation. In the short time available you have to be selective in the material to put in the talk. It is impossible to condense a 20 000 word dissertation to include everything into 15–30 minutes. This means you have to decide early on what to keep. The key points to mention would be the general aims of the research, how you went about it and why. This could be followed with a summary of the main conclusions and discussion. It would be difficult to mention all the literature, although you could note any particular piece of research similar to yours. You may also have the opportunity to refer to the literature at the end when people ask questions, especially if any particular author supports and agrees with your results and ideas. Check with your supervisor about the assessment regulations – they may give guidance as to the type of material to include in the presentation.

Format of a presentation

A presentation is best divided into five parts:

- Introduction
- Main part
- Conclusion
- Summary
- Question time

Introduction

Here you introduce the talk and also yourself. Outline the various topics in the order you are going to talk about them, and if you are using handouts give them out. Try and establish a relationship with the audience. Even though you know them quite well, standing up and speaking in front of them is a different situation. Adopt a formal, but friendly manner.

Main part

Here you describe the main information about your presentation. Keep to the same order as given in the introduction, and tell the audience when you have finished one section and are going on to the next. If you are using visual aids explain them thoroughly to the audience. Students often prepare excellent visual aids but never use them to full advantage. They only refer to them quickly and carry on talking about the next topic. This is confusing to the audience. They are not sure whether to look at the visual aid or listen to you. It is also wasteful of your time and effort. Remember, if you are nervous, when using a visual aid the audience is looking at it and not at you. Your time is limited, so pick any examples with care. It is better to explain a few carefully, than skim superficially through several. This will only leave the audience confused, and possibly bored.

Conclusion

Here you describe your conclusions. Again a visual aid can be used to list the salient points.

Summary

It is a good idea to finish with a short summary highlighting the major topics described. When reading a book readers can always go back to remind themselves of what has gone before, an audience can't do this, they rely on the speaker to tell them. Again a visual aid at the end summarizing the main points is a good idea.

Question time

Here the audience has the opportunity to ask questions about your dissertation. The sort of questions will be similar to those listed above with respect to a *viva*. When answering questions be honest. If you don't know the answer say so. The advice about answering questions is the same as that for a *viva*.

Preparing for a presentation, including the use of visual aids

As with all your work sound preparation is the best way to achieve a good and professional result. Go through your dissertation picking out the points you want to include in the talk. As noted above, time is limited so you must be selective, whilst ensuring relevant assessment criteria are met. Use the material you feel most confident with and, if possible, anything that you felt was different and sets your dissertation apart from other students. Write yourself some notes to take into the presentation. The essential thing is to write notes not a script. Never read out loud or learn by heart (unless it's a quotation) what you want to say. It will sound stilted and most likely you will speak too quickly. Make the writing large so you can see your notes from a distance. Never be note bound and scared to take your eyes off the writing – it will mar your delivery. Some people have their notes on cards rather than paper. Use whichever you prefer. It is a good idea to have the sheets numbered in order just in case they get mixed up. If you are going to use visual aids then make a mark in the notes when you will need them.

The best preparation for a presentation is practice! Stand up in an empty room and speak out loud what you want to say. Talk at a steady pace sorting out the pronunciation of any difficult words. Time yourself and if you over-run but you think the pace is about right, then think what you can take out. It's a good idea to rehearse a presentation a number of times. It all helps to achieve an excellent result. As you practise you may make changes in your notes. If your notes begin to look untidy, providing you can understand them, this is fine. However, if you think the alterations and changes confuse you, and you would be more confident with neater notes, then copy them out.

Visual aids

It is always a good idea to include some visual aids in a talk. PowerPoint is mostly used, and is an excellent package. However, don't overload each slide with too much information. Keep it simple. It is possible with PowerPoint to achieve very clever effects, but remember it is the information that is important. Five or six lines of writing are enough, together with any graphics you might want to use. Handouts summarizing the main points you want to make are excellent, and each member of the audience can take a copy away with them. Quite often a handout is a copy of the PowerPoint presentation, although you may want to add extra information in order to provide a more complete picture.

Final preparation and delivery

There comes a point when you have to stand up and deliver your talk. The following advice will help:

- Check that the room is ready, the seating is how you want it and the computer and any other equipment is in working order, and you know how to use it.
- Wear comfortable clothes. A presentation is not the time to wear a new pair of uncomfortable shoes. Try and remain calm and relaxed. Even experienced presenters are apprehensive at the start. Channel the nervous energy into giving a good talk.
- Talk to the entire audience not just to the examiner, or one particular member of staff. Look at all the people present in the room, keeping eye contact.

This helps to establish a relationship with the audience. Speak slowly, clearly, not too loud and project your voice to the back of the room so everyone can hear.

- Be interested and enthusiastic about your dissertation. If you sound bored, the audience soon will be.
- Keep the language simple, and explain any unusual or technical term. Refrain from telling jokes.
- Stand rather than sit when giving a presentation. Standing gives you more command of the situation. You can see the audience better and notice if they appear not to understand any part. Use the audience's reactions – if they are looking bored you can speed up the delivery or slow down if they are looking confused. Keep reasonably still – don't move around, and don't stand in front of the screen when using a visual aid.
- Don't try to hide your notes. You are not expected to give a presentation from memory. As you talk have a quick look to see what comes next. Use your notes as a prompt.
- All speakers at some point make a mistake in a presentation. They get lost, get material out of order, or miss out something important. If this happens don't panic – tell the audience by saying for example 'I'm sorry, I've just realized I've missed out an important point, can we start from ...'. The audience will understand and be quite happy to accept the apology.

Summary

This chapter has looked at the processes involved in the assessment of dissertations. The key points in this chapter are:

- How dissertations are marked at undergraduate and postgraduate level, including the use of assessment criteria.
- The role of the *viva* in the assessment of dissertations.
- The points to note if you have to give a presentation as part of the assessment.

11   Specialist subject advice

Introduction

This chapter provides some information on a variety of popular subjects associated with business and management. The aim is not to provide detailed accounts of marketing, strategic management and the like, but present a series of key points that could form the basis of a dissertation. Note that many subjects are inter-related, for example, finance and human resource management are relevant to most, if not all, aspects of business. Also in recent years the concepts of ethical and corporate responsibility have become more significant and can form part of many dissertations. Examples of potential dissertation titles are also given. The depth of treatment for each one would depend whether they formed part of an undergraduate or postgraduate course.

Marketing

KEY POINTS

- Marketing strategy, research and forecasting
- Product life cycle, development and innovation
- Positioning and dominance in the market
- Distribution and logistics
- Advertising, brand management and loyalty marketing
- Promotions
- Pricing and retail issues
- Marketing economics
- International marketing

POTENTIAL DISSERTATION TITLES

An investigation into the marketing of non-profit-making organizations with special reference to a well-known charity.

A comparative study of marketing theory and the actual marketing of a youth employment training scheme. An evaluation of its success or failure.

An investigation into the factors influencing successful sport sponsorship, using a well-known breakfast cereal as a case study.

The role of the advertising agency and their relationship with the car industry, with reference to the family car.

Strategy and policy-making

KEY POINTS

- The nature of strategy and strategic planning and policy-making
- The formulation and implementation of policy
- Integration and expansion strategies
- Competitive strategies
- The effect on people – negotiation and communication
- Globalization and strategic planning
- Different models of strategy
- The value of 'vision' and 'mission' statements

POTENTIAL DISSERTATION TITLES

An investigation into the strategy of business process management with respect to small and medium sized enterprises.

An analysis of the development of the corporate strategy of a named multinational company. The role played by senior management.

> *The part played by middle management with respect to changes in corporate strategy in two similar sized organizations. An experimental approach.*
>
> *How to globalize – an examination and comparison of two successful companies.*

Finance and accounting

KEY POINTS

- Financial strategies and business plans
- Control of fiscal policies
- Incentives to staff and other stakeholders
- Financial planning – short and long-term
- Budgetary control and the banking industry
- Investments – political and social implications
- Financial decision-making
- Mergers and acquisitions – government interventions

POTENTIAL DISSERTATION TITLES

> *An investigation into the factors involved when two companies merge with reference to the roles of senior staff.*
>
> *A comparative study of the banking services provided today with those of 20 years ago.*
>
> *The Acme Building Society: an examination of its success from its start in 1902 until the present day.*
>
> *An investigation into the financial implications of introducing a customer loyalty card programme with reference to a high street pharmaceutical chain.*

Human resource management

KEY POINTS

- Appraisal, rewards and performance management
- Leadership versus management
- Equal opportunities
- The importance of minorities
- Self-development: its place in a contemporary company
- Job design – the successful recruitment of staff at all levels
- Skills and competencies – their identification, measurement and role
- The role of teams – supervising and leading teams

POTENTIAL DISSERTATION TITLES

An investigation into the function of the human resources department of a named company with respect to the needs of middle management.

Are leaders born or bred? An investigation into the characteristics of leadership with reference to a large media company.

Self managing teams: an assessment of their formation and function. A case study approach.

A critical examination of the recruitment policies adopted by small companies when employing MBA graduates.

Resource management

KEY POINTS

- The need for an information system
- Technological innovation and the role of IT
- R&D and resource management
- The design and implementation of a management information system
- What is information and why is it needed? Its storage and retrieval
- Principles of management information systems
- How to put resource management into practice

POTENTIAL DISSERTATION TITLES

An introduction to electronic data exchange: a study of the factors involved with respect to a named company.

An evaluation of an introduction of management information systems into a small, traditional, family-run business.

The introduction of a computerized system into a predominantly paper-based personnel office, 15 years on: An examination of the success or otherwise, and the effect on the company.

An evaluation of the factors influencing resource management in information-based organizations. A case study approach.

Managing change

KEY POINTS

- Innovation and change. Why is change necessary?
- The factors involved in managing change – political factors
- Change at a department and company level
- Strategies to implement change and cope with change
- The introduction of change – the stages involved
- Communicating change to staff and customers
- Staff development issues

POTENTIAL DISSERTATION TITLES

Managing change in the National Health Service: a case study approach.

An evaluation of changes in higher education policy with respect to a named 'new' university in the UK.

Culture and change management: an investigation of the need for change in a named organization.

The management of conflict – an investigation into the role and responsibility of senior management during the implementation of change.

Total quality management

KEY POINTS

- What is TQM?
- Standards – national and international issues
- Factors influencing the introduction of TQM
- The effects on the client within a customer focused organization
- The effects on the staff – the influence of senior management
- The meaning of quality
- Audits on quality
- Total quality control

POTENTIAL DISSERTATION TITLES

An analysis of the implementation of TQM within the leisure industry.

Quality audits: a study into the factors influencing their success or otherwise in a named public sector organization.

Benchmarking: its role with respect to TQM in a public sector organization. An investigative study.

An examination of the factors that may influence the implementation of total quality control in a manufacturing company.

International business

KEY POINTS

- Globalization – competing in a global market
- The ethical, environmental and political implications of international activities
- The EU and its implications for the UK
- Managing people and the influence of different cultures and language
- Communication across frontiers
- International competition
- Financial considerations
- The importance of information technology and global business
- Managing a global business

POTENTIAL DISSERTATION TITLES

A comparative study showing how the image of a multinational company changes from country to country.

An investigation into selected worldwide brands and their impact on the global market.

A case study investigation of the problems faced by a named small company when they try to enter the global market place.

An evaluation of the effectiveness of a worldwide advertising campaign used by a named international hotel group.

Ethics and business

KEY POINTS

- The social responsibility of companies
- The role of stakeholders
- Environmental and 'green' issues, e.g. pollution, toxic and other waste disposal
- The role of the individual vs the role of the organization
- The philosophical framework of ethics in business
- Social and political influences

POTENTIAL DISSERTATION TITLES

The ethics of fundraising – an investigation into the practices of a large named charity.

An evaluation of the marketing of genetically modified foods with reference to cereal crops – is this an ethical or business problem?

An assessment of the advantages and limitations that a socially responsible company face in today's competitive environment with reference to the oil industry.

A critical examination of managerial ethics with respect to the pharmaceutical industry.

Facilities management

KEY POINTS

- Management of personnel – need for special training
- Health and safety issues
- Legal responsibilities
- Mechanical maintenance
- Electrical maintenance
- Maintenance of grounds and buildings
- Energy conservation
- Financial implications

POTENTIAL DISSERTATION TITLES

A comparative study of the role of the facilities management director in a large private company and a public/state controlled department.

An investigation into the need for an effective facilities management policy in a named small manufacturing company.

An investigative study into the training needs of facilities management staff: the use of 'in-house' versus 'off-site' providers.

The introduction of wind turbines to supply and supplement a company's energy needs – an ethical study into the management of such a project.

Entrepreneurship and new venture creation

KEY POINTS

- What is entrepreneurship?
- Its history and development
- The entrepreneurial process
- The need for a viable business plan
- Entrepreneurial leadership and management
- Searching for venture capital
- Recognizing and utilizing potential opportunities
- Ethical implications
- Successful vs unsuccessful companies

POTENTIAL DISSERTATION TITLES

The characteristics of a successful entrepreneur – a case study approach.

An analysis of a successful entrepreneurial company: an investigation into the entrepreneurial process.

'Successful entrepreneurial companies can grow and expand very quickly'. An examination of the factors influencing the management of very rapid growth.

A study of the role of teams in an entrepreneurial organization.

E-business

KEY POINTS

- What is e-business – its history and development
- The economics of e-business
- Technological aspects – the increasing role and applications of e-technologies
- E-business and staff – social and behavioural issues
- Its suitability for all or some companies
- The organization and management of e-business
- Digital marketing
- Ethical and regulatory issues

POTENTIAL DISSERTATION TITLES

An investigation into the future, challenges and opportunities of e-business with respect to a large retail chain.

Project management and e-business: An examination of the factors involved using a named organization as a case study.

An examination of the special skills and training needed by e-business staff. A senior management perspective.

An investigation into how the role of a CEO in an e-business enterprise is different from that in a more traditional business environment.

12 Glossary

The following terms, arranged in alphabetical order, are all associated with research and the production of a dissertation. The list is not exhaustive, but hopefully it may provide some additional help to you when working on your dissertation.

A

Abscissa (*plural* abscissae) This is the horizontal axis of a graph, and is termed the x axis. The independent variable is plotted on this axis.

Abstract A concise summary of a research article or paper. An abstract should highlight the key points of the research, but be complete in its own right. Some publishers advise that it should be no more than 5 per cent of the total word count. Abstracts are also found at the beginning of a dissertation, and it is one of the last things you write.

Academic integrity It is essential that all aspects of any research (including the actions of the researcher) are carried out with a commitment to all ethical considerations and follows any prescribed protocols, e.g. university guidelines.

Academic style Academic writing is normally very formal, written in the third person and includes accepted referencing styles to acknowledge other people's work. In certain situations, depending on the topic, a more informal style is adopted. Professional publishers normally have a 'house style' which writers are expected to follow.

Action research This is where the researcher is an interventionist, and the research is linked to a plan of action to cause a change, which in turn hopefully brings about an improvement. Action research is cyclic and uses a number of techniques to collect data and information.

Alternative hypothesis Referred to as H_1 this hypothesis implies that something special has happened, and a statistical significant change has taken place. See also null hypothesis.

Analysis of variance (ANOVA) A parametric statistical method to investigate how much variability can be the result of different causes. There are a number of variations of this analysis. The one to use depends on the nature of the investigation being carried out.

Analytical induction This is the second stage of keeping a research diary.

The descriptions and actions recorded in the diary are worked through, and themes and ideas are identified.

Assessment　See formative and summative assessment.

Assessment criteria　These are like standards against which academic work is judged. In order to reach the required standard the work needs to meet and satisfy the criteria.

Axes　Graphs have two axes at right angles to each other. They are the *y* or vertical axis (termed the ordinate) and the *x* or horizontal axis (termed the abscissa). They meet at the origin of the graph, which is zero on both axes.

Axiology　This is the study of value and goodness, and is closely related to ethics and aesthetics.

B

Bar charts　These, like graphs, have data set against two axes, and are best used when one set of variables is non-numerical. The data is displayed using rectangles, all of the same width. The length of each is proportional to the frequencies they represent. They can be drawn in several ways, e.g. a vertical bar chart, horizontal bar chart, component bar chart, and back-to-back bar chart.

Bias　When collecting information from a sample you need the sample to be truly representative of the population, and have no special characteristic(s). The characteristic(s) can be termed bias. It can be caused by a number of things, such as a poor sampling frame, a poor interviewer etc.

Bibliography　A list of published information sources, arranged alphabetically normally by author's surname, giving full publication details of each source.

Binomial distribution　This is a frequency distribution where only two mutually exclusive outcomes are possible, e.g. loss or gain, heads or tails if you were tossing a coin.

C

Case example(s)　This is an alternative term for vignettes.

Case study　This is an extensive research study of a single situation, e.g. individual, family, organization. It uses a number of techniques to collect information and data. There are different types of case studies, including typical, atypical, precursor and multiple case studies.

Categorical (nominal) data　This is data that can be put only into one category, e.g. make of car. It is essential that the categories are quite distinct, and data cannot be put into more than one.

Census　A test or count where every member of the population is involved.

Chi-square (or χ^2) test　This is a statistical test where the observed result is compared with the expected result. The test uses nominal data. The chi-square test can also be used to determine whether an observed distribution of data fits a particular known distribution, e.g. normal, Poisson, etc.

Citation record   This is where in academic writing, e.g. research paper, text book, another author is referred to in the text. Publishers have different 'house styles' of citing references – check with your university regulations what they expect in your dissertation.

Closed question   A question used in a questionnaire that can only have one answer, e.g. yes or no.

Cluster analysis   A non-linear method using separate pieces of paper, e.g. 'Post-it' notes to generate ideas. Each idea is written on a separate sheet, and then ordered and classified at a later stage.

Cluster sampling   A method of non-random sampling where members of the sample are chosen from one or several groups (or clusters).

Coding   This is used in questions where descriptions are given. The descriptions need to be given a numerical value, so they can be analyzed. If done by hand it takes time and needs a consistent approach.

Cognitive mapping   This is a specialized group interview that takes place in an action research setting.

Column graph   A special type of bar chart that only uses discrete data. Each column in the graph is kept separate.

Computer assisted qualitative data analysis systems (CAQDAS)   This is specialized computer software used to evaluate and interpret the results of qualitative research. A number of packages are now on the market.

Content analysis   This method is used in qualitative research where there are a lot of descriptions and narrative accounts. The frequency of particular key words, ideas and concepts are identified and counted. Content analysis is sometimes termed textual analysis.

Continuous data   This is data that can take any value, e.g. the amount of flour milled in a factory can be of any weight. Continuous data is measured not counted.

Control(s)   This is used in experimental research where the effect of a particular treatment is measured in some way. The control situation is not subjected to the treatment.

Covert observation   This is where in an observation situation the researcher remains anonymous to all other people within the observation setting. The researcher's identity is not revealed.

Critical incident technique   This is used in an interview situation where the interviewee is asked to describe and/or discuss a specific incident that they regard as critical, and which may have brought a significant change to their lives with respect to the research being carried out.

Critical reflection   This is where the researcher constantly re-visits the basic ideas about the research and reflects on what is happening and what they want to achieve. This continual looking back at a research problem helps the researcher to clarify their thoughts and ideas.

Critical sampling A special type of purposive or judgemental sampling, where there is a controversial or contentious issue(s) being researched.

Critical thinking When carrying out a piece of research it is important to relate the research and its interpretation to work that has been done before. Critical thinking implies that the researcher's work is linked to that of others so that points of similarity and difference are identified.

Crystallization Some researchers now prefer this term as an alternative to triangulation.

D

Data triangulation A type of triangulation where the data is collected from different sources over different time periods.

Deductive research This is research that is quantitative in approach and uses the scientific method. A hypothesis is set up, and depending on the results obtained it is either accepted or rejected.

Dependent variable This is used in experimental research, and whether a change in one factor (the independent variable) produces a change in another factor (the dependent variable). The independent variable is the variable which is not affected by changes in the other variable, i.e. it is independent. The dependent variable can be affected by changes in the other.

Descriptive observation This is the first part of the process of keeping a research diary where all activities and events about the research are first recorded. This is followed with analytical induction.

Descriptive statistics The analysis and display of research data in simple mathematical terms. It usually involves the production of tables, charts, figures and diagrams.

Diary(ies) This is a good method of recording research data and information. It is very useful with observational methods of research. The keeping of a diary by the researcher is useful for all types of research, and is a great help at the writing up stage.

Discrete data This is data that increases in complete steps or jumps, for example chickens can only lay 1, 2, 3 eggs, etc. They cannot lay 1½ eggs. Discrete data is counted, not measured.

Dispersion This is sometimes called variation, and is the pattern that a particular characteristic takes when spread across the population. The mean height of men in a population provides no information whether there is a large number of tall or short men; it only gives you the average height. It doesn't give any information about the dispersion or variation of height in the population.

Dissertation format Dissertations are written up in a very formal style. They are divided into headed sections or chapters. Universities normally provide guidelines as to how they expect students to write up their work.

Distribution(s) Characteristics of populations often follow a particular pattern or distribution within the population, e.g. normal, binomial or Poisson. The type of distribution governs the type of statistical testing that can be applied.

E

Epistemology This is the study of knowledge, and how it affects the world in which the researcher lives.

Ethics This is concerned with the principles and values that are involved with any research. Ethics implies honesty and integrity, not only in the way the research is carried out, but also in the way the research is written up and presented.

Ethnography This is a distinctive qualitative methodology involving the direct observation of a particular research situation. It can also use a number of quantitative techniques depending on the research being carried out.

Experiment A method of research where changes are deliberately made and any resulting observations are recorded and measured. Experiments investigate the relationship between cause and effect. In theory the researcher should be able to control all the factors involved in an experiment, but in practice this is difficult to achieve.

Extreme sampling A type of purposive sampling where there is the need to

focus on somewhat different and unusual issues.

F

Fish bone diagram These are also called Ishikawa diagrams after their creator Kaoru Ishikawa. They are used in the manufacturing industries, and in quality control to explore solutions to problems. They are called fish bone diagrams because they look like the skeleton of a fish. They help in creative thinking and in the generation of new ideas. Software packages are now available which will generate the diagrams for you.

Flow chart A diagram showing how the changes in a process lead from one to another. Figure 5.1 illustrating stages in survey design is an example of a flow chart. They are useful in sorting out ideas, and arranging them in a logical order.

Focus group This is a group interview situation, and the interviewer (or moderator) guides and prompts the discussion with a selected group of people.

Formative assessment This is where all the student's work on a course and their total learning experience is assessed. The final grade achieved is not solely dependent on final examinations or the like. Educational researchers often discuss the advantages and disadvantages of this type of assessment.

G

Graphs This is a diagram showing the relationship between two variables. There are different types of graph, e.g. semi-log graph, and a number of mathematical properties that can be applied in some situations.

Grounded theory This idea was first presented by Glaser and Strauss (1967). It is associated with qualitative research. A particular theory or idea arises from the data that is collected by empirical research. The researcher does not have any pre-conceived ideas at the start of the research, and treats the material collected as a whole, constantly reflecting to refine any theory that develops from the data.

H

Harvard system This is a well-established and widely recognized system of citing references. There are slight variations in the way in which publications are listed. Always follow any university guidelines you are given.

Hawthorne effect This is a term that is now used in experimental research following the work of Mayo (1933) at the Western Electrics Hawthorne site, Chicago, US between 1927 and 1932.

Heterogenous sampling Used mainly in purposive sampling where there is the need to identify a range of topics. Samples are chosen so they can provide a variety of information.

Histogram This is a chart that displays group data. The width of each bar is proportional to the class interval and the area of each bar is proportional to the frequency it represents.

Homogenous sampling This is where samples are more or less the same. It is used in purposive sampling.

Hypothesis This is where a theory is put forward, and following an investigation the theory or hypothesis is either accepted or rejected. The term is used mainly in scientific based research. The word here has a different meaning from when used in statistical analysis. See null or alternative hypotheses.

Hypothetico-deductive This is a term used mainly in conjunction with quantitative research. The hypothesis is put forward, and following the research, theories are deduced.

I

Idiographic research This term is used to describe research that is subjective, i.e. that is qualitative in approach.

Independent variable See dependent variable.

Inferential statistics This is a branch of statistics that uses hypothesis testing and statistical tests of significance. Some tests are mathematically complex and specialist help is often needed.

Indirect observation This is information that may be present in an observational research setting that the researcher may come across, such as information on noticeboards, internal memos, overheard conversations etc.

Intellectual property   A patent is an intellectual property. It is where an invention, new process, or something similar is protected legally against unauthorized copying and counterfeit. On a global scale the policing of an intellectual property can be difficult to enforce.

Interval data   This is where a scale is used and there are equal distances between points on the scale, e.g. temperature. There is no true zero with interval data.

Interview   This is where the researcher questions someone (the interviewee) about some aspect of the research in question. Interviews need to be well planned and organized beforehand.

Investigator triangulation   This is where a number of researchers observe and record the same event at the same time. This is not normally possible with undergraduate work, but may be possible with postgraduate research.

Isotype   Also termed pictographs, this is an effective way of displaying data. It uses symbols to represent the subject being studied. Selecting appropriate symbols can be difficult and an isotype is not suitable for small numbers, e.g. 6, 7 and 9 etc.

J

Judgemental sampling   See purposive sampling.

L

Learning agreement/contract   This is an agreement between the student and the university as to exactly what each will contribute to the learning process. In some institutions they can be very formal; in others they can be less so. The important point about learning contracts and agreements is that they aim to make the student more responsible for their own learning.

Likert scale   A term used to describe ranking questions used in questionnaires. The scale is used if you want to gauge a degree of opinion about a subject.

Lorenz curve   A special graph that shows inequalities with certain subjects like income levels, manufacturing outputs, etc. The cumulative percentages of a population (e.g. companies) are plotted against the cumulative percentages of the variable being studied (e.g. employment).

M

Mann-Whitney U test   A non-parametric test used for two samples drawn from the same population. The test uses ordinal data.

Mature knowledge   This is concerned with well-established theories, concepts and ideas about a particular topic. Any new research carried out with respect to the topic mainly reinforces established ideas and theories.

Mean This is the arithmetic average. It is defined as the value each item in a distribution would have if all the values were distributed and shared equally.

Median This is the value of the middle item in a distribution.

Methodological fit This involves the researcher deciding what would be the best way to investigate a particular topic, and involves deciding on the particular methodological approach and the best techniques to use.

Methodology Not to be confused with the word method, methodology is the overall approach the researcher takes to investigate a particular subject. It aligns with the philosophical basis on which the research is founded.

Method(s) These are the individual techniques used to collect data. Note that method and methodology are not the same.

Method triangulation This term is used in conjunction with research and the concept of triangulation. It is where the researcher uses a mix of qualitative and quantitative methods.

Mind mapping This is a non-linear way to come up with ideas and suggestions about a subject. The emphasis is to try and think creatively and be as unstructured as possible.

Mixed knowledge This is a topic being researched which involves a mixture of nascent and mature knowledge.

Mixed methods research This is where the researcher investigates a problem using a number of different methodological approaches. It produces a lot of data about a subject, but

can be time consuming and may be more appropriate for postgraduate work.

Mode This is defined as the value that occurs most frequently in a distribution.

Moderator In a group interview situation the interviewer is sometimes termed the moderator.

N

Nascent knowledge This implies new and novel ways to look at a situation. It is concerned with ideas and theories that are somewhat tentative and may be original with respect to a particular situation.

Nominal data Also termed categorical data, this is where the data is put into one category, e.g. makes of car.

Non-numerical data This is data collected in the form of descriptions. For any statistical analysis it needs to be coded into numerical data (see coding).

Non-parametric tests These tests make no assumptions about the population, and the data collected does not belong to any particular distribution.

Non-participant observation In this situation the researcher remains detached, and observes and records everything they see. They do not play any active role in the setting they are investigating.

Non-probability (non-random) sampling See non-random sampling.

Non-random (non-probability) sampling This occurs where it is difficult to determine an accurate sampling frame, and because of the nature of the research topic the sampling needs to be more subjective.

Non-response bias   This is bias that is introduced into the research by people, for whatever reason, not responding, e.g. the non-return of questionnaires.

Normal distribution   An example of a particular distribution within a population. The distribution is continuous in that if you were to measure the height of people, some would be very tall, some would be very short, but the majority would be somewhere in-between.

Null hypothesis   This is used in statistical tests of significance. The null hypothesis, referred to as H_0, states that for the test being carried out no special differences have occurred, and therefore no significant differences exist. See also alternative hypothesis.

Numerical data   This is data that is collected in number form. Note that numbers alone have little value; they need to be defined by a particular unit, e.g. height, weight, time, etc.

O

Observation   This is a popular research technique where a topic is viewed and observed by the researcher who records everything they see and hear. There are different types of observational research.

Observational schedule   This is a checklist of points to note when carrying out observational research.

One-group, pre-test, post-test, design   A form of experimental design where a sample group is pre-tested before the treatment and tested following the treatment. No control or comparison group is used.

One-shot case study   With this form of experimental design the subjects involved are subjected to a treatment and then measured. No control or comparison group is used.

Ontology   This is a branch of philosophy which is concerned about the nature of existence. It is important with respect to qualitative research which tends to be subjective as opposed to objective.

Open question   This is a question that asks for opinions and views about a particular subject. It can't be answered by 'yes' or 'no'. The replies need to be sorted and coded before they can be subjected to any form of analysis.

Ordinal data   This is data that is on a scale and has both classification and rank. It can only be used in certain types of statistical tests.

Ordinate   This is the vertical or y axis on a graph. See axes.

Overt observation   This is an observation setting where the researcher is known to all people involved in the research.

P

Paradigm   This is a difficult concept to explain. With respect to research it can be described as a set of assumptions, concepts, values and practices that make up a way of looking at the world within a particular academic discipline. With qualitative research, which is subjective, the researcher collects observations and descriptions of situations. With quantitative research, which is objective, the researcher collects numerical data which can be subjected to analysis.

Parametric tests of significance   A test that assumes the population has a particular form of distribution e.g. normal, binomial, etc.

Participant observation   In this instance the researcher is completely involved, and becomes part of the situation being observed and researched.

Pictograph   See isotype.

Pie chart   This is a simple but effective way to illustrate data. The data is arranged in a circle like a pie.

Pilot study   This a trial run or rehearsal of your research to test out your selected methodology, data collection and analysis methods. A pilot study alerts you to potential problems.

Plagiarism   This is where you try and pass off someone else's work as your own. Remember, with proper referencing and acknowledgement you can use and quote other people's work.

Poisson distribution   A particular type of distribution within a population. It occurs where a number of rate occurrences happen in a long series of trials, e.g. accidents at a busy road junction.

Population   The entire collection of items, individuals, etc. from which a sample is taken.

Positivism   This term is involved in quantitative research, and is normally associated with 'the scientific method'.

Pre-test, post-test, control group design   A more robust type of experimental design. Groups are tested at the start, where one group receives a treatment, the control does not. Both groups are then tested at the end of the experiment.

Primary information source/material   This is information that is new and original at the time of publication. It is found in refereed research articles and papers published in academic journals, conference proceedings, etc.

Probability   A measure of the likelihood of a particular event happening. The symbol for probability is p, and is measured from 0 to 1. Probability 0 implies impossibility, and probability 1 means that something will definitely happen.

Probability (random) sampling   This is where each member of the sampling frame has an equal chance of being selected. It works best with an accurate up-to-date sampling frame.

Proposal   A written up plan detailing a piece of research. It should include as much information as possible, including methodology, data collection techniques, proposed method of data analysis, resources needed, time scale, etc.

Purposive sampling   Sometimes called judgemental sampling, because the researcher selects a sample that they consider will provide the best information for the research topic in question.

Q

Qualitative methodology This approach to research argues that it is difficult, or even impossible, to be objective in a research situation, and in some instances the researcher is even part of the research. With this type of research the information collected is nearly always in the form of descriptions.

Qualitative research Qualitative research is subjective and does not involve an objective way of looking at things. The information collected is usually in the form of descriptions.

Quantitative methodology This is a research approach that aims to be objective. It is sometimes described as scientific, and always involves the collection and testing of numerical data in some way.

Quantitative research This research involves numerical data, which is then subjected to some form of analysis.

Quasi experiments A form of experimental design often used in business and management and other subjects like psychology. Its main difference from a traditional experimental approach is that it lacks features such as the random allocation of groups and proper controls.

Questionnaire A number of questions arranged in a particular order sent to a number of people to collect information about a particular topic(s).

Quota sampling A way of sampling often used in market research surveys where a number of interviewers are used. The interviewer has a particular number or quota of interviewees to find, but normally the choice of who to ask is left to the discretion of each interviewer.

R

Random (probability) sampling See probability (random) sampling.

Ratio data Ratio data is similar to interval data in that there are equal distances between points on the scale, but with ratio data there is also a true zero.

Relevance trees This technique, often used in strategic planning, divides a topic into small, discrete areas. It helps with creative thinking and is often used in technological forecasting.

Replacement sampling This is where in random sampling a sample can be used more than once. 'Without' replacement is where each sample may not be used more than once, and a second sample is selected.

Research design This is the overall plan for a piece of research. It includes the methodological approaches used, methods of data collection and subsequent analysis.

Research intention This is a short statement describing exactly what is the purpose and reason for a particular piece of research.

Research objectives/questions These are the precise questions you want to ask about the topic you are researching. Try and make them as clear cut as possible.

Research proposal   This is a detailed account of how the researcher intends to research a particular topic. A proposal, for example, should include details of methodology, research techniques, collection and analysis of data. Some mention of relevant literature should also be included.

Research rationale   This is an account which lists the reasons for carrying out a piece of research.

Research reliability   This is all about consistency and being true to your selected methods of research. It implies that another researcher could use your design and methods and repeat your work. They may get similar results, but their conclusions from the results may be different from yours.

Research statement   See research proposal.

Researcher bias   This is bias unwittingly introduced by the researcher. You may ask the wrong or badly worded question in an interview. A pilot study should help reduce this type of bias.

S

Sampling frame   The population from which you collect your sample is termed the sampling frame.

Sampling frame bias   This is bias caused by using an inaccurate, out-of-date sampling frame.

Sampling units   These are the individuals within a population that could form part of the sample used in an investigation.

Scientific method   This is the 'classical' way to conduct scientific research. A hypothesis is set up and following an experiment, the hypothesis is either accepted or rejected. In reality, scientific research is not so clear cut, and often a compromise has to be taken.

Secondary information source/ material   This is information that is not original in the sense that it has been published somewhere before. Material in textbooks tends to be secondary. It does provide, however, good background material for a dissertation.

Semi-log graph   With this type of graph the values of the dependent variable (y axis) are plotted using log numbers. If plotting the graph by hand you need either special graph paper or log tables. Note that 0 has no log, so don't put 0 on the vertical scale.

Significance test(s)   These are statistical tests that provide a measure of probability (p) whether the results are due to chance alone or because real differences exist.

Sign test   A non-parametric test of two matched samples drawn from the same population. It uses nominal data.

Simple random sampling   Sampling where each member of the population has an equal probability of being selected.

Static group comparison   This is a method of experimental design. Two groups are used. One is subjected to a treatment, the other is not. The group not treated acts as a kind of control.

Stratified random sampling   This is where the population can be divided into layers or strata, and samples are chosen randomly from each stratum.

Student's *t* test A test used to compare means of small samples, usually less than 30.

Summative assessment This is assessment carried out at the end of a programme. The grade the student achieves is normally awarded as a result of the final piece(s) of assessed work. As with formative assessment, education researchers hold opposing views as to the merits or otherwise of summative assessment.

Survey(s) An investigation of one or more variables of a population.

Systematic random sampling This is where the population is arranged into some sort of order. It is used when the sampling frame is large, for example, suppose in a population of 1 000 a sample of 100 is required, then every tenth person would be selected. The starting point for the first sample is chosen at random.

T

***t* test** See Student's *t* test.

Tests of significance Tests that are carried out to indicate whether a situation has occurred by chance alone, or that real differences exist. A level of probability (*p*) can be applied as a result of a particular test.

Theoretical triangulation A form of triangulation where the theory of one academic discipline is applied to another discipline. This is difficult in

business and management, which encompasses a number of different subjects like economics, finance and sociology.

Triangulation A general term that implies a research topic has been studied by a number of different methodologies and approaches. It is argued that if the same subject is viewed from different perspectives then a greater understanding should be achieved.

V

Validity The research design should fully address the research in that it should be true and valid. Any findings should be honestly collected, analyzed and reported.

Vignette This is a literary device for illustrating some aspects of a research topic. It is mainly used with qualitative research. A vignette can be described as a short account of an hypothetical situation where a research participant described their perceptions, beliefs and understanding, etc. about a particular situation.

Viva voce An oral examination, sometimes used in certain Masters programmes, and nearly always used at Doctorate level.

W

Wilcoxon signed rank test A non-parametric significant test, which uses ordinal data and matched pairs of scores from the same population.

X

x axis   This is the horizontal axis of a graph. The independent variable is plotted on this axis.

Y

y axis   This is the vertical axis of a graph. The dependent variable is plotted on this axis.

Z

Z chart   A special graph that extends over one year, and plots (i) individual monthly figures, (ii) monthly cumulative figures for the year in question, and (iii) a moving annual total. When plotted the three lines together look like the letter Z.

13 Annotated bibliography

The following texts have been selected in case you need extra help with certain parts of your dissertation. From experience, students have found them easy to follow and understand. Publication details for each were correct at the time of writing, but it's always worth checking to see if more recent editions are available. Although some titles are a little dated, the books themselves are still worth a look. Some titles are now available as e-books. Note that new books are coming out all the time so be aware of new stock arriving in the library. If there is anything in particular to highlight about a book a comment is made. All book and print references cited in previous chapters are also listed here.

General research books

A number of general texts on various aspects of research are on the market. They all cover the basic topics like proposals, data collection, writing up and the use of literature.

Biggam, J. (2011)
Succeeding with your Master's Dissertation: A step-by-step Handbook (2nd edition)
Maidenhead: Open University, McGraw-Hill Education

There is lot in this good book – it has an excellent section on plagiarism.

Blaxter, L., Hughes, C. and Tight, M. (2010)
How to Research (4th edition)
Buckingham: Open University Press

Burns, R.B. (2000)
Introduction to Research Methods
London: Sage

Denscombe, M. (2010)
The Good Research Guide for Small-Scale Social Research Projects (4th edition)
Buckingham: Open University Press

Fowler, F. (2001)
Survey Research Methods
Thousand Oaks, CA: Sage

Hoffmann, A. (2013)
Research for Writers (7th revised edition)
London: A. & C. Black

Although written for the professional writer, this book contains lots of useful advice about collecting information. Well worth a look.

Johnson, D. (1994)
Research Methods in Educational Management
London: Longman

Although written for the education market there are easy-to-follow chapters on most aspects of research, including action research and case studies.

Johnson, P. and Duberley, J. (2000) *Understanding Management Research.* London: Sage

Lomas, R. (2011) *Mastering your Business Dissertation: How to conceive, research, and write a good business dissertation* London: Routledge

Marshall, P. (1997) *Research Methods: How to Design and Conduct a Successful Project* Plymouth: How to Books

A small book, but it is well indexed and there is a useful glossary. There are good chapters on sampling and analyzing data.

Sharp, J. A., Howard, K. and Peters, J. (2001) *The Management of a Student Research Project* (3rd revised edition) Aldershot: Gower

This book contains good sections on the use of literature, data collection and analysis.

Thomas, G. (2009) *How to do your Research Project: A Guide for Students in Education, and the Applied Social Sciences* London: Sage

An easy to read book with lots of good advice.

Walliman, N.S.R. (2000) *Your Research Project: A Step-by-Step Guide for the First-time Researcher* London: Sage

White, B. (1991) *Studying for Science: A Guide to Information, Communication and Study Techniques* London: E. & F. N. Spon

This is an old book and although written for science students, there are lots of sections on general study skills. Chapter 2 has a section on reading techniques.

Business and management research books

There are a number of titles that specialize in the areas of business and management research methods.

Churchill, G.A. (Jnr) (1995) *Marketing Research: Methodological Foundations* (6th edition) Fort Worth: The Dryden Press

Churchill, G.A. (Jnr), Brown, G.A. and Churchill, T.J. (2004) *Basic Marketing Research* Fort Worth: The Dryden Press

Crainer, S. (1999) *Key Management Ideas: Thinkers that Changed the Management World (Management Masterclass)* (3rd edition) London: Financial Times, Prentice Hall

Easterby-Smith, M., Thorpe, R. and Jackson, P. (2012) *Management Research: An Introduction* (4th edition) London: Sage

Gill, J. and Johnson, P. (2010) *Research Methods for Managers* (4th edition) London: Sage

Kennedy, C. (2007) *Guide to the Management Gurus* (5th edition) London: Randon House Business

Quinlan, C. (2011) *Business Research Methods* Andover: Cengage Learning EMEA

Saunders, M., Lewis, P. and Thornhill, A. (2012)
Research Methods for Business Students (6th edition)
London: Financial Times, Prentice Hall

Thietart, R.A. (2001)
Doing Management Research: A Comprehensive Guide
London: Sage

Qualitative and quantitative books

The following are useful if you need particular help with specific techniques.

Balnaves, M. and Caputi, P. (2001)
Introduction to Quantitative Research Methods: An Investigative Approach
London: Sage

Bannister, P., Burn, G., Burman, E., Parker, I., Taylor, M. and Tindall, C. (2011)
Qualitative Methods in Psychology: a Research Guide (2nd edition)
Buckingham: Open University Press

Don't let the title put you off. There are excellent chapters on observation, interviews, and action research. Each chapter is well referenced.

Creswell, J.W. (1994)
Research Design: Qualitative and Quantitative Approaches
Thousand Oaks, California: Sage

Creswell, J.W. (2008)
Educational research: Planning, conducting, and evaluating quantitative and qualitative research (3rd edition)
NJ: Prentice Hall

Creswell, J.W. (2013)
Research Design: Qualitative, Quantitative Approaches, and Mixed Methods (4th edition)
London: Sage

Written for the postgraduate market there are useful sections on overall design and experiments.

Denzin, N.K. and Lincoln, Y.S. (eds) (2011)
The SAGE Handbook of Qualitative Research (4th edition)
London: Sage

This contains a wealth of information about the techniques available.

Duignan, J. (2014)
Quantitative Methods for Business Research Using Microsoft® Excel®
Andover: Cengage Learning EMEA

Glaser, B. and Strauss, A. (1967–1976)
The Role of Grounded Theory
Chicago: Aldine

Munn, P. and Dreyer, E. (2004)
Using Questionnaires in Small Scale Research: A Teacher's Guide
Edinburgh: The Scottish Council for Research in Education

Although written for school teachers, this is an excellent guide covering all aspects of questionnaire research.

Ritchie, J. and Lewis, J. (eds) (2003)
Qualitative Research Practice: A Guide to Social Science Students and Researchers
London: Sage

Robson, C. (1993)
Real World Research
London: John Wiley & Sons

Silverman, D. (1999)
Doing Qualitative Research: A Practical Handbook
London: Sage

Literature books

The following titles should help when handling the literature.

Hart, C. (2001)
Doing a Literature Search: A Comprehensive Guide for the Social Sciences
London: Sage

A good book and will help when handling the literature.

Oliver, P. (2012)
Succeeding with Your Literature Review: A Handbook for Students (Open up Study Skills)
Buckingham: Open University Press

Ridley, D. (2010)
The Literature Review: A step-by-step Guide for Students
London: Sage

Statistics books

The titles below are useful if you need additional help with quantitative analysis. Most of them give worked examples of the various tests of significance you may need.

Blaikie, N. (2003)
Analyzing Quantitative Data: From Description to Explanation
London: Sage

Fielding, J. and Gilbert, N. (2006)
Understanding Social Statistics
(2nd edition)
London: Sage

A well-written and easy to follow book.

Harper, W.M. (1998)
Statistics (Framework series)
(6th edition)
London: Financial Times, Prentice-hall

This is an excellent book, and has good sections on the drawing of tables and figures.

Malim, T. and Birch, A. (1997)
Research Methods and Statistics
London: Macmillan

Although written for psychology students, this is a very easy book to read. There are some excellent sections on how to carry out the statistical tests.

Sirkin, R.M. (2005)
Statistics for the Social Sciences
(3rd edition)
London: Sage

This is a very detailed text, and is easy to read.

Waters, D. (2011)
Quantitative Methods for Business
(5th edition)
London: Financial Times, Prentice Hall

Wright, D.B. and London, K. (2009)
First (and second) Steps in Statistics
(2nd edition)
London: Sage

Writing up books

The following give advice about the writing up stage and associated issues.

Bryson, B. (2009)
Troublesome Words
London: Penguin

An excellent book – it covers all the pitfalls about spelling and grammar.

Legat, M.L. (1989)
The Nuts and Bolts of Writing
London: Robert Hale

Although published a number of years ago this is a useful little book with easy-to-follow chapters on punctuation, spelling and style.

Lester, J.D. (Jnr) and Lester, J.D. (late) (2011)
Writing Research Papers: A Complete Guide (International Edition)
(14th edition)
London: Pearson

This contains lots of material and there is a useful guide on using and citing information.

Swetnam, D. and Swetnam, R. (2000)
The Bestselling Guide to Planning, Preparing and Presenting First Class Work (3rd edition)
Oxford: How to Series Books

Other book and print references cited

Balnaves, A. and Teddlie, C. (2010)
Handbook of Mixed Methods in Social & Behavioral Research
London: Sage

Basit, T.N. (2003) 'Manual or electronic? The role of coding in qualitative data analysis'
Educational Research, 45(2), 143–154

Bassey, J. (1999).
Case Study Research in Educational Settings (Doing Qualitative Research in Educational Settings).
Buckingham: Open University Press

Baugh, J.B., Hallcom, A.S. and Harris M.E. (2010)
Computer Assisted Qualitative Data Analysis Software: a Practical Perspective for Applied Research.
Revistga del Instituto Inernacional de Costos, No. 6.

Blank, G. (2004)
'Teaching Qualitative Data Analysis to Graduate Students'
Social Science Computer Review, 22, 187–196

Directory of British Associations and Associations in Ireland (20th edition)
Beckenham: CBD Research Ltd

CBD Research Ltd publish lists and details on a number of topics – search them out online.

Edmondson, A. and McManus, S.E. (2007)
'Methodological Fit in Management Field Research'
Academy of Management Review, 32(4), 1155–1179

Elliott,J. (1980)
Action Research in Schools: Some Guidelines
Classroom Action Research Network Bulletin no 4.
Norwich: University of East Anglia

Finch, J. (1987)
'The Vignette Technique in Survey Research'
Sociology, 21, 105–114

Friedmann, X. (2011)
The World is Flat: The Globalized World in the Twenty-First Century
Leipzig, Germany: Klett Ernst/Schulbuch

García-Horta, J.B. and Guerra-Ramos, M.T. (2009).
'The use of CAQDAS in educational research: Some advantages, limitations and potential risks'
International Journal of Research & Method in Education, 32(2), 151–165

Grogan, C. and Brett, J. (2006)
Google and the Government of China: A Case Study in Cross-Cultural Negotiations
Evanston, Ill: Kellogg School of Management.

Halsey, A.H. (ed). (1972)
Educational Priority: Volume 1: E.P.A. Problems and Policies.
London: HMSO

Heifetz, R.A., Linsky, M. and Grashow, A. (2009).
The Practice of Adaptive Leadership: Tools and Tactics for Changing Your Organization and the World.
Boston, MA: Harvard Business Press.

Hodgkinson, G.P. (ed). (2001)
'Facing the Future: The Nature and Purpose of Management Research Re-assessed.'
British Journal of Management, 12, Special Issue.

Hwang, S. (2008).
'Utilizing Qualitative Data Analysis Software. A review of Atlas.ti'
Social Science Computer Review, 26(4), 519–527

Kenyan, I. (2009)
Collective Memory and Intergroup Leadership: Israel as a Case Study
Harvard Business Press Chapters: HBS Press

Lester, R. (2013)
Libraries and Information Sources in the UK and Republic of Ireland 2013–2014 (38th edition)
London: Facet Publishing

Lester, R. (ed) (2007)
Walford's Guide to Reference Material (9th edition)
London: Facet Publishing

Lewins, A. and Silver, C. (2007)
Using Software in Qualitative Research
London: Sage

Lowe, R. and Gilligan, C. (1995)
Revitalising the SME Sector through Focused Building Support Strategies.
British Academy of Management Annual Conference, 1995. Conference Proceedings, Sheffield, UK pp. 13–21.

Macmillan, K. and Koenig, T. (2004).
'The Wow Factor: Preconceptions and Expectations for Data Analysis Software in Qualitative Research'
Social Science Computer Review, 22, 179–186

Mayo, E. (1933)
The Human Problems of an Industrial Civilization
London: Macmillan

Mintzberg, H. (1973)
The Nature of Managerial Work
New York: Harper and Row

O'Hare, C. (2007)
Business Information Sources: A Beginner's Guide
London: Facet Publishing

Ozanne, J.L. and Saatcioglu, O.B. (2008)
'Participatory Action Research'
Journal of Consumer Research, 35(3), 423–439

Plant, R. (2013)
Treat Everything as a Case Study. Harvard Business Review Blog Network. Accessed at http://blogs.hbr.org/cs/2013/01/treat_everything_as_a_case_study.html on the 28th February, 2013.

Rapoport, R.N. (1970)
Three Dilemmas in Action Research
Human Relations, 23(6), 499–513

Richards, T. (2002).
An intellectual history of Nud*ist and NVivo
International Journal of Social Research Methodology, 5(3), 199–214

Sandberg J. and Targama, A. (2007).
Managing Understanding In Organizations
Sage: London

Tashakkori, A. and Teddlie, C. (2010)
Handbook of Mixed Methods in Social and Behavioural Research.
London: Sage

Thompson, V. (2013)
Encyclopedia of Business Information Sources (2 vol set)
London: Gale Cengage

Zaccaro, S.J. and Klimoski, R.J. (eds) (2002)
The Nature of Organizational Leadership: Understanding the Performance Imperatives Confronting Today's Leaders
NY: Jossey Bass

Index